WITHDRAWN

REFERENCE GUIDES IN LITERATURE
Marilyn Gaull, *Editor*

Robert Southey:
A Reference Guide

Kenneth Curry

G. K. HALL & CO., 70 LINCOLN STREET, BOSTON, MASS.

Copyright © 1977 by Kenneth Curry

Library of Congress Cataloging in Publication Data

Curry, Kenneth.
　　Robert Southey,: a reference guide.

　　(Reference guides in literature)
　　Includes index.
　　1.　Southey, Robert, 1774-1843--Bibliography.
Z8828.43.C86　　　[PR5467]　　016.821'7　　　76-51435
ISBN 0-8161-7831-3

This publication is printed on permanent/durable acid-free paper
MANUFACTURED IN THE UNITED STATES OF AMERICA

TO RICHARD BEALE DAVIS

COLLEAGUE AND FRIEND

Contents

Introduction ix

List of Abbreviations xv

Writings by Robert Southey xvii

Writings about Robert Southey, 1796-1975 1

Doctoral Dissertations 85

Author/Subject Index 89

Introduction

Robert Southey's works received many critical notices during his lifetime, many of them politically inspired. Although most of this criticism was only hastily composed journalistic reviewing, several serious essays - or chapters in well-known books - now occupy a place in nineteenth-century critical writing. Such are Francis Jeffrey's review of Thalaba in the first issue of the Edinburgh Review (1802), the chapter on Southey in Coleridge's Biographia Literaria (1817), the description of Southey and his library in Thomas De Quincey's Recollections of the Lake Poets (1839), Hazlitt's assessment in his Spirit of the Age (1825), Macaulay's famous attack upon the Colloquies in the Edinburgh Review (1830), and Carlyle's description and tribute to Southey in his Reminiscences (1881). After Southey's death his life and work received less attention, and much of the attention which he did receive was in general histories of literature or in biographies of his more celebrated contemporaries. Indeed, it was not until thirty-six years after his death that the first scholarly biography, written by Edward Dowden, appeared, utilizing the ten volumes of amorphous material from Cuthbert Southey's Life and Correspondence of the Late Robert Southey (1849-50) and the collection of letters edited by Southey's son-in-law, J. W. Warter (1856). Victorian essayists such as George Saintsbury, Leslie Stephen, and John Dennis also noticed Southey as a writer of importance. It was not, however, until the twentieth century that Southey and his work began to receive scholarly attention in a search for sources and influences and in establishing the canon of his writings. William Haller's book on the early life and work of Southey (1917) and Zeitlin's series of articles identifying Southey's contributions to the Critical Review (1918) are notable examples of the beginning of this new emphasis. Within the last half century further substantial book-length studies have appeared in the form of biography, editions of unpublished travel journals, annotated editions of published works, and bio-critical estimates of Southey's achievement: examples of these are Simmons' Southey (1945), Cabral's edition of the Portuguese journals, Cabral's study of Southey and Portugal, Carnall's Robert Southey and His Age, Raimond's Robert Southey: L'homme et son temps, and Curry's Southey in the Routledge Author Guide Series. Since the publication of Cuthbert Southey's Life and Correspondence and Warter's four-volume edition of selected letters, Edward Dowden published Southey's correspondence with Caroline

Robert Southey: A Reference Guide

Bowles and P. B. Shelley (1881), and letters both from and to Southey have appeared in scores of books and articles, but the most important new collection was the two-volume publication of New Letters of Robert Southey in 1965.

Critical judgments on Southey's works fall into several easily recognizable patterns that have changed very little since his own day. Most critics agree in valuing his prose more highly than his poetry although he is popularly remembered as a poet and as a poet laureate. Such prose works as his biographies of Nelson and Wesley receive high marks, and many critics have also a good word for the Espriella Letters (Letters from England by Don Manuel Espriella). His Colloquies receive praise from twentieth-century historians who admire his insight into the problems of the day and his recommendations for improvement; however, this book received on its publication a devastating criticism from Macaulay who, convinced of the correctness of the Whig laissez-faire economic doctrine, objected to Southey's recommendation of governmental "interference" in matters of social welfare and education. In this instance posterity appears to be on the side of Southey. The histories, on the whole, have few apologists, but some writers maintain that they still contain examples of vivid narrative and the biographical sketches reveal again Southey's talent for biography. Southey's one attempt at fiction, The Doctor, has had a mixed reception, some call it a delightful bedside book and its discursiveness part of its charm, but others think the whole thing a bore. Opinion here seems about equally divided. "The Story of the Three Bears" contained in the fourth volume is universally admired even if Southey's most severe critics may declare it to be his only claim to remembrance. Among all his writings Southey's letters have received the most universal approval from the Lockhart-Elwin review in the Quarterly (1850) of Cuthbert Southey's Life and Correspondence to the judgments of Leslie Stephen, W. M. Thackeray, and M. H. FitzGerald. The poems, however, have not fared so well. Although Jeffrey's attack on Thalaba praised some aspects, Jeffrey objected to the new school of poetry of which it was an example. The long narrative poems are usually disapproved of as a group, but almost every critic will select one of the five for praise, if often qualified praise. Roderick is generally considered Southey's finest largely because of its nearness to everyday experience; the characters are seen as real, and the setting in Spain had a topical interest which was, because of the recent war in the Iberian Peninsula, familiar to the ordinary reader. Joan of Arc was admired on publication (1796) for its revolutionary sentiment, and Hazlitt (1825) still thought it the best of the five. Madoc is generally conceded to be the least interesting, but Thalaba is admired and preferred by Lockhart and Elwin, and The Curse of Kehama by Saintsbury and Simmons.

If critics find it difficult to be enthusiastic about the long narratives, most still find a good word for the ballads, an occasional sonnet, and a few short lyrics. "The Battle of Blenheim" is so often quoted and reprinted that it appears to be the most frequently anthol-

Introduction

ogized of all Southey's poems. The most popular of Southey's ballads - where the grotesque and horrible are humorously combined - were nearly all written during the years 1798 to 1800 when he served as Daniel Stuart's laureate to the Morning Post at a guinea a week: to this period belong "The Old Woman of Berkeley," "Cornelius Agrippa," "Bishop Bruno," "The Well of St. Keyne," "The Inchcape Rock," and "Queen Orraca." The lyrics, "The Holly Tree," "Books," and "The Cataract of Lodore" and an occasional sonnet such as "To a Goose" and "Winter" still find sympathetic and appreciative readers.

Overall estimates of Southey are not wanting. Indeed, many of the biographical-critical essays are very general and offer sweeping judgments rather than detailed analyses. Southey has never wanted for staunch supporters who make stout claims for his importance as a representative man of letters - here Saintsbury and Dowden stand out among Victorian scholar-critics as Landor had stood out among Southey's own generation. Others, however, find no - or very little - good to say of any thing about Southey either of his work or of his personality. Such depreciatory judgments reached a low point in 1909 and 1913 with the essays of Symons and Lounsbury. Two other sweeping condemnations of Southey appeared in the two anonymous leading articles in the Times Literary Supplement in 1943 and 1945.

Almost every literary history, encyclopedia, or biographical dictionary has something to say about Southey in the form of a biographical sketch, a grouping of his works, and a general estimate of his stature and importance. This Reference Guide does not list these general sources except for the work of Elton (1912), Saintsbury (1914), and Bernbaum (1949) since these accounts represent essays by scholars who were widely read and knowledgeable about Southey's biography and works. Social and intellectual histories of the nineteenth century - as well as literary histories - often contain a section or a chapter on Southey such as Beer (1919), Brinton (1926), and Schilling (1946). These discussions, however, usually emphasize the Espriella Letters and the Colloquies, although they sometimes draw upon the correspondence.

In addition to general estimates of Southey and his works many articles add importantly to our knowledge of specific works: such articles are those on his Specimens of the Later English Poets (1945), his Annual Anthology (1948), his periodical contributions to the Critical Review (1918), the Annual Review (1939), the Foreign Review and the Foreign Quarterly Review (1932), and the Quarterly Review (1949, 1975). Hoadley's article on Wat Tyler (1941) gives a full account of that work and its various pirated printings. Havens' article on the Life of Wesley (1946), based upon the original manuscript, gives valuable information. Our knowledge of Southey's Spanish and Portuguese studies has been enhanced because of the work of Ludwig Pfandl (1913) and Adolfo Cabral (1959, 1960).

ROBERT SOUTHEY: A REFERENCE GUIDE

The beginning student of Southey has several readily available guides. First, there is the very full listing of materials by Geoffrey Carnall in the New Cambridge Bibliography of English Literature. Then, for an elementary introduction, the chapter in Ernest Bernbaum's Guide Through the Romantic Movement (1949) is useful. My essay on Southey in English Romantic Poets and Essayists: A Review of Research (1957, revised, 1966) offers evaluative judgments and commentaries upon editions, bibliography, biography, and critical studies. The student interested in the correspondence will find the notes to my edition of New Letters of Robert Southey (1965) together with the biographical sketches of Southey's chief correspondents valuable, and my article, "The Published Letters of Southey: A Checklist," in the Bulletin of the New York Public Library (1967) lists 144 sources of letters. The present volume records all the later publication of letters after 1967.

Some selectivity of entries has been imperative since reviews and assessments of Southey have appeared continuously for almost 180 years. From the contemporary reviews of Southey which evaluated his individual works on their publication a representative and generous selection has been made. All notices of his works that appeared in the three major critical journals of the early nineteenth century - the Edinburgh Review, the Quarterly Review, and Blackwood's Edinburgh Magazine - are listed since these periodicals wielded the greatest influence to the largest audience. A sampling from the less celebrated periodicals has also been included. The emphasis in this Reference Guide, however, is upon the posthumous critical and scholarly attention accorded Southey and his works because this area is the one in which the student needs information and guidance. Here I have tried to be inclusive and to list all full-length articles and books that make even a modest contribution to Southey scholarship or criticism. I have not, however, cited every item from Notes and Queries or from the correspondence columns of the London Times Literary Supplement since these notes usually add little or nothing to our knowledge of Southey and his works. I have also excluded articles that only reprint a letter or two since that information is available in my article in the Bulletin of the New York Public Library (1967.B1). Articles of substance that include unpublished letters are, however, cited for the information and discussion contained in the articles. Book reviews, except for an occasional review-article, are also excluded.

Three useful works can be advantageously used in connection with this Reference Guide. Lionel Madden's Robert Southey: The Critical Heritage (1972.A1) reprints extracts and occasionally complete reviews of Southey's works from 1794 to 1879; Madden also reprints allusions to Southey from diaries and letters of nineteenth-century authors. John O. Hayden in The Romantic Reviewers 1802-1824 (1969.B3) has a perceptive essay on the reception of Southey's works during that period and an appendix which lists the reviews of his works for those years. William S. Ward in Literary Reviews in British Periodicals 1798-1820 (1972.B3) duplicates some of the material in Hayden's appendix but has some entries not in Hayden.

Introduction

A few contemporary notices of Southey less well known than those by Jeffrey, Hazlitt, Coleridge, and Carlyle may be mentioned here for their out-of-the-way points of view. John Foster's review of Kehama (1811.B4) takes quite serious exception to the poem because it treats seriously a pagan religion which is not, according to Foster's theology, true. William Taylor's reviews are distinguished by his highly original style of which a quotation is given from his review of Thalaba (1803.B3). John Wilson's review of The Doctor in Blackwood's (1835.B1) is not odd, but it is a charming essay in itself for a reader who is familiar with the book because Wilson writes his review in the manner of The Doctor - but without telling the reader he is so doing. The conclusion of Herman Merivale's review of Southey's collected poetical works (1839.B2) observes Southey's fascination with violence and destruction, a point not often made in criticism of Southey but one which could be explored. Thomas Lister in his review in the Edinburgh Review of Southey's Lives of the Uneducated Poets (1831.B1) observes that Southey estimates too highly the value which the uneducated derive from writing poetry. Such persons should rather be encouraged to pursue a mechanical and more "practical" occupation and not be encouraged to rise above their rank in society. By focusing attention on such persons Southey is in a sense subverting the class structure of society!

The pattern of the review during Southey's age was a rigid one. The usual review summarized the work and quoted lengthy extracts, and the critical comment - if any - was confined to a sentence or two of censure or commendation often related more to the political or religious affiliation of the periodical rather than to any fixed literary principles. The nine reviews by Jeffrey of Southey's works and the two by Macaulay are thus exceptions to the rule. The persistence of the old style - which was being broken in the Edinburgh, Quarterly and Blackwood's - is found in Heber's reviews of Southey's History of Brazil in the Quarterly and in the anonymous review in Blackwood's of A Tale of Paraguay in which the reviewer summarizes and quotes hundreds of lines of the poem - so many that a reader would not need to turn to the original.

The contemporary reviews of Southey's works were unsigned, but the identity of many of the reviewers is now known. I am indebted to the following sources for the names of the reviewers listed in the Reference Guide. The reviewers in the Edinburgh Review, Blackwood's Edinburgh Magazine, and the Quarterly Review (after 1824) are identified by Walter E. Houghton, The Wellesley Index to Victorian Periodicals 1824-1900 (University of Toronto Press, 1966) and in the Quarterly Review before 1824 by Hill and Helen Shine, The Quarterly Review Under Gifford: Identification of Contributors 1809-1824 (1949.B3). B. C. Nangle in The Monthly Review, Second Series, 1790-1815 (Oxford: Clarendon Press, 1955) has identified the reviewers to that periodical during that twenty-five year span. My identification of William Taylor's reviews is from J. W. Robberds' A Memoir of the Life and Writings of the Late William Taylor of Norwich (1843.B2), which lists

Taylor's reviews to the *Annual Review*, the *Monthly Magazine*, and the *Critical Review*. For information about James Montgomery's reviews I am indebted to John Holland's and James Everett's *Memorials of the Life and Writings of James Montgomery* (London, 1855).

List of Abbreviations

AL	American Literature
Archiv	Archiv für das Studium der Neueren Sprachen und Literaturen
BB	Bulletin of Bibliography
BC	Book Collector
BJRL	Bulletin of the John Rylands Library
BNYPL	Bulletin of the New York Public Library
CLQ	Colby Library Quarterly
DUJ	Durham University Journal
ELH	Journal of English Literary History
ES	English Studies
HLB	Harvard Library Bulletin
HLQ	Huntington Library Quarterly
JAF	Journal of American Folklore
JEGP	Journal of English and Germanic Philology
KSJ	Keats-Shelley Journal
LT	Levende Talen
MLN	Modern Language Notes
MLR	Modern Language Quarterly
MP	Modern Philology
MQ	Midwest Quarterly (Pittsburg, Kansas)
New Letters	New Letters of Robert Southey, ed. Kenneth Curry. New York: Columbia University Press, 1965. Two volumes.
N & Q	Notes and Queries
NLWJ	National Library of Wales Journal
PBSA	Publications of the Bibliographical Society of America
PMLA	Publications of the Modern Language Association of America
PQ	Philological Quarterly
PULC	Princeton University Library Chronicle
RES	Review of English Studies
RLV	Revue des Langues Vivantes (Bruxelles)
RR	Romanic Review
SB	Studies in Bibliography
SEEJ	Slavic and East European Journal
SGG	Studia Germanica Gandensia
SIR	Studies in Romanticism

SP	Studies in Philology
TLS	[London] Times Literary Supplement
TSL	Tennessee Studies in Literature
TWC	The Wordsworth Circle
YR	Yale Review
YULG	Yale University Library Gazette

Writings by Robert Southey

<u>Books</u> (place of publication is London unless otherwise stated)

<u>The Fall of Robespierre: An Historic Drama</u>. Cambridge, 1794. Coleridge wrote Act I: Southey, Acts II and III.

<u>Poems</u>, by Robert Lovell and Robert Southey. Bath, 1795.

<u>Joan of Arc, An Epic Poem</u>. Bristol, 1796.

<u>Poems</u>. Bristol. 1797; second edition, 1797.

<u>Letters Written During a Short Residence in Spain and Portugal</u>. Bristol, 1797. Revised 1799; Revised 1808.

<u>Poems</u>. 1799.

<u>Thalaba the Destroyer</u>. 1801.

<u>Madoc</u>. 1805.

<u>Metrical Tales and Other Poems</u>. 1805.

<u>Letters From England by Don Manuel Alvarez Espriella</u>. Reprint edited by J. Simmons, 1951 (<u>See</u> 1951.A1).

<u>The Curse of Kehama</u>. 1810.

<u>History of Brazil</u>. Vol. I, 1810; Vol. II, 1817; Vol. III, 1819.

<u>Omniana, or Horae Otiosiores</u>. 1812. With Coleridge. Reprint edited by R. Gittings, 1969 (<u>See</u> 1969.A1).

<u>The Origin, Nature and Object of the New System of Education</u>. 1812. Reprint. 1972.

Robert Southey: A Reference Guide

An Exposure of the Misrepresentations and Calumnies in Mr Marsh's Review of Sir George Barlow's Administration at Madras, by the Relatives of Sir George Barlow. 1813.

The Life of Nelson. 1813. Many reprints: ed. G. Callender. 1922 (See 1922.A1); E. H. R. Harvey. 1953 (See 1953.A1).

Roderick, the Last of the Goths. 1814.

Odes to His Royal Highness the Prince Regent, His Imperial Majesty the Emperor of Russia, and His Majesty the King of Prussia. 1814.

Carmen Triumphale, For the Commencement of the Year 1814. 1814.

The Minor Poems of Robert Southey. Reprints with some revision Poems, 1797, 1799, and Metrical Tales, 1805.

The Poet's Pilgrimage to Waterloo. 1816.

The Lay of the Laureate. Carmen Nuptiale. 1816.

Wat Tyler: A Dramatic Poem. 1817.

A Letter to William Smith, Esq. M.P. 1817.

The Life of Wesley; And the Rise and Progress of Methodism. 1820. Many reprints; ed. M. H. FitzGerald. 1925 (See 1925.A2).

A Vision of Judgment. 1821.

The Expedition of Orsua; And the Crimes of Aguirre. 1821.

The History of the Peninsular War. Vol. I, 1823; Vol. II, 1827; Vol. III, 1832.

The Book of the Church. 1824.

A Tale of Paraguay. 1825.

Vindiciae Ecclesiae Anglicanae. 1826.

All for Love; and The Pilgrim to Compostella. 1829.

Sir Thomas More; or, Colloquies on the Progress and Prospects of Society. 1829.

Essays, Moral and Political. 1832.

Lives of the British Admirals. Vols. I-II, 1833; Vol. III, 1834; Vol. IV, 1837. Reprinted as English Seamen, ed. D. Hannay, 1895, 1904 (See 1895.A1).

WRITINGS BY ROBERT SOUTHEY

Letter to John Murray, Esq. 'Touching' Lord Nugent. 1833.

The Doctor. Vols. I-II, 1834; Vol. III, 1836; Vol. IV, 1837; Vol. V, 1838; Vols. VI-VII, 1847. Many reprints. A selection edited by M. H. FitzGerald. 1930 (See 1930.A1).

The Life of the Reverend Andrew Bell. 1844. Vol. I by Southey; Vols. II-III by C. C. Southey.

Oliver Newman: A New-England Tale (Unfinished); With Other Poetical Remains. 1845.

Robin Hood: A Fragment. By the Late Robert Southey and Caroline Southey. Edinburgh. 1847.

Common-Place Book. Ed. J. W. Warter. Four vols. 1849-51.

Journal of a Tour in the Netherlands in the Autumn of 1815. Boston. 1902 (See 1902.A1).

Journal of a Tour in Scotland in 1819. Ed. C. H. Herford, 1929 (See 1929.A1)

Journals of a Residence in Portugal, 1800-1801 and a Visit to France, 1838. Ed. Adolfo Cabral. Oxford, 1960 (See 1960.A1).

Books Edited and Translated by Southey

On the French Revolution. By Mr Necker. 1797. Vol. II tr. by Southey.

The Annual Anthology. 1799-1800. Two volumes. Southey edited and contributed.

The Works of Thomas Chatterton. 1803. Three volumes. Ed. by Southey and Joseph Cottle.

Amadis of Gaul, by Vasco Lobeira. 1803. Four volumes. Tr. by Southey.

The Remains of Henry Kirke White: With an Account of His Life. 1807.

Palmerin of England, by Francisco de Moraes. 1807. Four volumes. Munday's translation corrected by Southey.

Specimens of the Later English Poets. 1807. Three volumes.

Chronicle of the Cid. 1808. Limited Editions Club, New York, 1958 (See 1958.A1).

Robert Southey: A Reference Guide

The Geographical, Natural, and Civil History of Chili, by J. Ignatius
   Molina. 1809. Two volumes. Annotated by Southey.

The Byrth, Lyf, and Actes of King Arthur, by Thomas Malory. 1817.
   Two volumes.

The Pilgrim's Progress, With a Life of John Bunyan. 1830.

Attempts in Verse, by John Jones, an Old Servant: With...An Intro-
   ductory Essay on the Lives and Works of Our Uneducated Poets.
   Reprint of biographies by J. S. Childers. Oxford, 1925 (See
   1925.A1).

Select Works of the British Poets, From Chaucer to Jonson, With Biographical Sketches. 1831.

Horae Lyricae. Poems...By Isaac Watts. With a Memoir of the Author.
   1834.

The Works of William Cowper...With a Life of the Author. 1835-37.
   Fifteen volumes.

The Poetical Works of Southey, collected by himself. 1837-38. Ten
   volumes. Many reprints.

Poetical Works With a Memoir of the Author. H. T. Tuckerman.
   Boston, 1860. Ten volumes. Many reprints.

Collections of Letters

The Life and Correspondence of the Late Robert Southey. Ed. C. C.
   Southey. 1849-50. Six volumes. (See 1849.A1).

Selections from the Letters of Robert Southey. Ed. J. W. Warter.
   1856. Four volumes.

The Correspondence of Robert Southey with Caroline Bowles. Ed.
   Edward Dowden. Dublin, 1881 (See 1881.A1).

New Letters of Robert Southey. Ed. Kenneth Curry. New York, 1965.
   Two volumes. (See 1965.A1).

Writings about Robert Southey, 1796-1975

1796 A BOOKS - NONE

1796 B SHORTER WRITINGS

1   AIKIN, JOHN. Review of Joan of Arc. Monthly Review, n.s. 19 (April), 361-68.
    Summarizes plot and quotes numerous passages. Predicts for Southey "a rich harvest of future excellence," but deplores evidence of haste in composition, incorrect pronunciation of French names, and the coinage of new verbs from nouns. The sentiments of the poem are of the present, not of the age of Joan, being "uniformly noble, liberal, enlightened, and breathing the purest spirit of general benevolence and regard to the rights and claims of human kind."

2   ANON. Review of Joan of Arc. Analytical Review, 23, 170-77.
    A suitable story for an epic. Reviewer admires, despite many imperfections, "the noble spirit of freedom, which is evidently the poet's inspiring muse; the ready invention, which has enabled him to embellish an historical narrative of narrow extent, with all the charms of fiction; the fertile fancy...the learning...the correct and elegant taste in versification."

1797 A BOOKS - NONE

1797 B SHORTER WRITINGS

1   AIKIN, JOHN. Review of Poems. Monthly Review, n.s. 22 (March), 297-302.
    Quotations from the poems lead to the recommendation of the book: "Genius is a despotic power, and irresistibly commands homage."

Robert Southey: A Reference Guide

1797

2 ANON. Review of Poems. Monthly Mirror, 3 (February), 102.
"The fertility of this writer's imagination is only equalled by the elegance of his taste." Commends the sonnets on the slave trade and "The Triumph of Woman," a paraphrase of some chapters in Esdras.

3 ANON. Review of Letters Written During a Short Residence in Spain and Portugal. Monthly Mirror, 4 (August), 97.
Writes on manners, literature, and political liberty "like a man of taste, information, and liberal sentiments."

1799 A BOOKS - NONE

1799 B SHORTER WRITINGS

1 ANON. Review of Annual Anthology. Vol. I. Monthly Mirror, 8 (September), 155.
Praises Southey's own poems especially his "Inscriptions." Most of the anonymously published poems "are below mediocrity" and reviewer hopes that Southey will "not permit his friendship to outrun his judgment" in future anthologies.

1801 A BOOKS - NONE

1801 B SHORTER WRITINGS

1 ANON. Review of Annual Anthology. Vol. II. Monthly Mirror, 11 (January), 32.
Anthology still contains too many "jejune productions." Southey's "Battle of Blenheim" has a "charming simplicity."

2 ANON. Review of Thalaba. British Critic, 18 (September), 309-10.
Objects violently to the versification: "this unharmonious stuff - which, were not the lines divided by the printer, no living creature would suspect to be even intended for verse." As for the work itself it is "Tales of Terror, run mad."

3 ANON. Review of Thalaba. Monthly Mirror, 12 (October), 243-47.
Wishes that the narrative and descriptive parts had been in blank verse and the lyrical parts in rhyme. Writer is a "real poet" but addicted to "affectation, puerility, and false English." Conclusion: "We recommend his beauties to the esteem, and his faults to the forgetfulness, of every reader."

1801 A BOOKS - NONE

1801 B OTHER WRITINGS

1   JEFFREY, FRANCIS. Review of Thalaba. Edinburgh Review, I, 63-83.
    This first, lengthy and serious estimate of Southey's poetry recognized that he belonged to "a sect of poets" who held a creed opposed to the then accepted standards of poetry. The essay-review is thus as much an attack upon Wordsworth, Coleridge, and Lamb as it is a review of Thalaba. Jeffrey finds in Thalaba the same "affectation of great simplicity and familiarity of language" as in Lyrical Ballads. The versification of Thalaba also comes under attack as hardly distinguishable from prose. The story of the poem - summarized at length - is called a series of "extravagant fictions" and one that "sets nature and probability at defiance." The copious notes to the poem indicate that the poem is often "little else than his commonplace book versified." Jeffrey, however, concludes that the poem does have passages of "very singular beauty and force" of which he quotes several examples including the opening lines. Although Jeffrey praises the author's "amiable mind" and "cultivated fancy" his faults are aggravated because of his adherence to this new school "of which he is a faithful disciple, and to the glory of which, he has sacrificed greater talents and acquisitions, than can be boasted of by any of his associates."

1803 A BOOKS - NONE

1803 B OTHER WRITINGS

1   ANON. Review of Amadis of Gaul. Monthly Mirror, 16 (November), 318-20.
    Gives general account of the romance and its importance. "Of the present version...it is impossible to speak in too high terms." Regrets that metrical pieces are given in Anthony Munday's translations.

2   SCOTT, WALTER. Review of Amadis of Gaul. Edinburgh Review, 3 (October), 109-36.
    Gives account of Amadis and of romance as a genre. Commends Southey for not following Tressan and Herberay "in the impure descriptions and obscenities which they have much oftener introduced, than found, in the Spanish original." Scott approves of Southey's abridgements in the

1803

> story, describes his style as resembling that of Froissart, but regrets his use of such phrases as "devilry," "Sir Knave," and "Don False One." Regrets that Southey did not provide his own translations of the sonnet-like poems in Amadis.
> Reprinted 1834.B1.

3 TAYLOR, WILLIAM. Review of Thalaba. Critical Review, 2nd ser. 39 (December), 369-79.
> Thalaba is not a metrical romance but a lyrical one, a story told by a series of pictures. Because the proper heroes of Thalaba are supernatural this supernatural quality "intercepts very much our fellow-feeling." Admires the style of Thalaba, which is described thus: "The favourite formulas of every school of diction have been acquired, and are employed. Many passages display the genitive substances and conjunctions-copulative of the Hebrew, many the picturesque circumstantiality of the Italian, and many the interjected onomatopeias of the German writers: less predilection is shown for the compound adjectives of the Greeks, for the sentences without particles of the Latins, or the abstract allegoric personifications of the English." Review concludes with a summary and lengthy quotations.

1804 A BOOKS - NONE

1804 B OTHER WRITINGS

1 SCOTT, WALTER. Review of Southey's and Cottle's Works of Thomas Chatterton. Edinburgh Review, 4 (April), 214-30.
> Retells Chatterton's life from the materials in the book. Disappointed that Southey did not write "a memorial of his ill-fated brother bard." Includes many quotations from Chatterton's poems and praises the two editors for their laudable efforts in devoting the proceeds to the benefit of the Chatterton family.
> Reprinted 1834.B1.

1805 A BOOKS - NONE

1805 B OTHER WRITINGS

1 ANON. Review of Madoc. Eclectic Review, 1 (December), 899-908.
> Finds "horror" to be Madoc's leading characteristic. Objects to strange names of characters, compound epithets

("dwindling our all-too-few"), and such odd words as "guidage" for "guidance." Concludes that Southey's unpardonable innovations upon his native language...deserve the severest reprehension."

2   ANON. Review of Madoc. Imperial Review, 5 (November), 465-73.
    Gives detailed summary of the plot, objects to the flatness of style and lack of "tropes, figures, and similitudes," but praises the story, the characters, and the sentiments. Calls the work "the second heroic production in the English language." Concludes that Southey's "muse is always devoted to the service of benevolence, justice, and humanity."

3   FERRIAR, JOHN. Review of Madoc. Monthly Review, n.s. 48 (October), 113-22.
    Objects to Southey's failure to follow Aristotle's rules for epic poetry and the strange names of the characters. Concludes that Southey's new method of writing "has failed to interest our feelings, or to excite our admiration."

4   JEFFREY, FRANCIS. Review of Madoc. Edinburgh Review, 7 (October), 1-28.
    Deplores Southey's failure to follow tradition. "In matters of taste, however, we conceive that there are no discoveries to be made, any more than in matters of morality," Jeffrey observes. Southey and his associates try for "singularity" and the result is "an affectation of infantine innocence and simplicity; an affectation of excessive refinement and preternatural enthusiasm; and an affectation of a certain perverse singularity in learning, taste, and opinions." Jeffrey suggests that if Southey would write in the measure of Dryden or Pope that practice would show him his own "exuberance and prolixity." Madoc is too long, but contains beautiful passages. "The radical blunder" of the story "consists in ascribing to a Welch chieftain of the 12th century the discoveries and exploits of the Spaniards 300 years later." To Madoc are accorded the exploits of Columbus and Cortez. Southey's style has instead of "elevation and originality" only "bombast and obscurity." But if Madoc cannot be admitted to the first rank, it contains nonetheless beautiful passages, which Jeffrey quotes at length - nine pages in all. The book itself is "one of the most elegant volumes that has lately issued from the British press."

1805

5   TAYLOR, WILLIAM. Review of Madoc. Annual Review, 4, 604-13.
      Echoes much of the review in the Monthly Magazine but makes additional points. The character Madoc "has much of the Washington: that practical good sense, which, when applied to selfish purposes, is denominated prudence; a reliance on justice and mildness, as the most stable grounds of authority; courage in its manliest form; and a little Welsh warmth, which occasionally betrays him into welcome indiscretion." Prefers the style of Thalaba to Madoc. "The author has been tamed by his critics, and Pegasus now moves in harness." Defends the poem from the common criticism of the oddity of the proper names.

6   _____. Review of Madoc. Monthly Magazine, 19 (July), 656-58.
      Summarizes the plot and concludes the poem is too long and could be condensed. Southey's style is "correct, not daring," and the descriptive passages are the most successful. "As a whole, the censure of Madoc is difficult; one must make a grievance of the levelness of manner, of the extent of narration, and of the absence of the wonderful, in order to provide the hostile converser with topics of invective." Concludes that since Paradise Lost "no poem has quitted the English press equal in merit to Madoc. It is a great and a durable accession to our literature."

7   _____. Review of Metrical Tales. Annual Review, 4, 579-81
      Thinks Southey should not have published so much. "The poetic rank to which he aspires, would long ago have been conceded, had he laid before us only the specimens of his excellence." "The Old Woman of Berkeley" is pronounced "the best original English ballad extant."

1807 A BOOKS - NONE

1807 B OTHER WRITINGS

1   ANON. Review of Specimens of the Later English Poets. Annual Review, 6, 557-60.
      A work of this type is not really wanted since most of the writers are deservedly forgotten. Several of Southey's biographical introductions (on Nahum Tate, James Miller, James Thomson, for example) are quoted in full.

2   [BROUGHAM, HENRY (?).] Review of Specimens of the Later English Poets. Edinburgh Review, 11 (October), 31-40.
      Object of the publication is not clear. "We have closed his volumes with the disappointment of perceiving, that nine tenths of his poets so denominated, have no visible title to such a name; and, that, in almost every instance,

1808

his selections from the real tribe of Parnassus, are specimens of their secondary, if not of their worst compositions." No evidence that works reprinted here represented the taste of the day. Despite these blemishes, Sir William Blackstone's "The Lawyer's Farewell to the Muse" and Bamfylde's "Cold is the senseless heart," are favorably mentioned.

3   TAYLOR, WILLIAM. Review of Letters from England. Annual Review, 6, 637-42.
    Summary and extensive quotation. Observes that the Spanish mantle is well made up, but the "English frock frequently peeps out from under the cloak."

1808 A BOOKS - NONE

1808 B OTHER WRITINGS

1   ANON. Review of Chronicle of the Cid. Annual Review, 7, 91-99.
    Praises introduction and notes. Summarizes the work.

2   ANON. Review of Palmerin of England. Annual Review, 7, 575-85.
    Discussion and summary of poem. Concurs in Southey's view that the author is Francisco de Moraes.

3   JEFFREY, FRANCIS. Review of Letters from England by Don Manuel Alvarez Espriella. Edinburgh Review, 11 (January), 370-90.
    Does not attribute authorship to Southey, but recognizes the book as from "the pen of a practised writer." Best passage is the account of an excursion to the Lakes. Objects to minute descriptive detail of household articles and means of traveling. The author, who is a defective reasoner, is a member of the "sentimental" rather than the "reasoning class of composers." Complains that his description of the condition of the inhabitants of the manufacturing towns is "highly coloured" and that the author querulously observes all institutions but suggests no scheme for improvement. Concludes by praising author's "laudable zeal for freedom and love of peace."

4   MOODY, CHRISTOPHER LAKE. Review of Letters from England. Monthly Review, n.s. 55 (April), 380-86.
    Attributes work to Southey and Richard Duppa, who have "over-acted their part" since no foreigner could possibly have such an intimate acquaintance with English literature, arts, politics, and sects. Objects to overemphasis upon

1808

religious sects. But Don Manuel does deliver shrewd comments on much medical and sectarian "mountebankery and fanaticism."

1809 A BOOKS - NONE

1809 B OTHER WRITINGS

1   ANON. Review of Chronicle of the Cid. Gentleman's Magazine, 79 (March), 236-45.
    Summarizes the work and praises the notes which are "uniformly pertinent, explanatory, and abound with the result of much patient research."

2   SCOTT, WALTER. Review of Chronicle of the Cid. Quarterly Review, 1 (February), 134-53.
    Summarizes the life of the Cid. Finds the faults of the work to be in the style, which is too scriptural, too periphrastical, and the unnecessary repetitions that derive from the metrical romance. Praise for the introduction and notes which are full and come "from works of equal curiosity and scarcity."
    Reprinted 1834.B1.

1810 A BOOKS - NONE

1810 B OTHER WRITINGS

1   ANON. Review of the History of Brazil. Eclectic Review, 6 (September), 788-800.
    The history of Brazil is not important enough to deserve so much labor and detailed description. Southey does not show here the "comprehensive views of the great philosopher" that are necessary for a great historian, and does not provide the reader assistance "in generalizing the phaenomena of savage life."

2   HEBER, REGINALD. Review of the History of Brazil. Quarterly Review, 4 (November), 454-74.
    Gives brief account of the history of Brazil with emphasis upon the savage tribes and the missionary efforts of the Jesuits. Objects to Southey's "occasional quaintness, and affectation of the style of antiquity" in contrast to the "polish" of the historian Robertson. The other defect "but which is a real impediment, not only to the general popularity, but to the general usefulness of an historical composition" is "the want of broad and general

views of his subject, and of those bird's-eye recapitulations, which serve as a resting place to the attention, and bring at once before the reader's observation the relative harmony of the objects he has gone through in detail."

1811 A BOOKS - NONE

1811 B OTHER WRITINGS

1 ANON. Review of The Curse of Kehama. Critical Review, third series 22 (March), 225-51.
  Objects to the unfamiliarity of the subject matter of the poem, the fact that there is "no leading point of interest in the story," and to the failure of the versification. Concludes that Southey "might be a great poet were the single gift of judgment to be added to the qualities which he undoubtedly possesses."

2 ANON. Review of the History of Brazil. Gentleman's Magazine, 81 (May), 458-60.
  Short summary of the history. Quotes title of books on South America which Southey would like to borrow for his future studies. "The narrative is written in a pleasing style, and it is embellished with many incidents explanatory of men and manners."

3 ANON. Review of The Curse of Kehama. Satirist, 8 (February), 168-74; (March), 249-56.
  A satirical-humorous summary of the plot of the poem stressing its incredulity and concluding "that amongst the various curses heaped on Ladurlad, though condemned to bear, he was not condemned to read the 'Curse of Kehama.'"

4 FOSTER, JOHN. Review of The Curse of Kehama. Eclectic Review, 7 (March), 185-205; (April), 334-50.
  First section of the review summarized the plot and quoted extensively. The critical second part objects to the fictions of Kehama on the ground of its defiance of the known laws of the universe and because of its favorable presentation of a false, pagan religion. "The whole affair of the operation of the Curse, the story of Lorrinite, the origination of the Ganges, the fire and water palace of Indra, the adventures of Mount Calasay, the transactions and creatures of Padalon...are things of a nature not only in perfect contrariety to the state and laws of the actual creation, but incompatible with any economy of which we can

1811

conceive the <u>possible</u> existence." Objects to the "irreverence" of the poem in describing as true a pagan religion, and asks if the poet sought "to render false gods and their worship...<u>agreeable</u> objects to the reader's imagination, and as far as possible <u>interesting</u> to his affections?" Concludes that Southey cannot be acquitted of the charge. Although the language of the poem is praised ("we have repeatedly exulted in the capabilities of the English language"), the versification "is a complete defiance of all rule."

5   JEFFREY, FRANCIS. Review of <u>The Curse of Kehama</u>. <u>Edinburgh Review</u>, 17 (February), 429-65.

An introduction observes that the judgments of posterity are usually in accord with contemporary judgments and then notes that no one of Southey's three long poems has really succeeded with a large number of readers. Southey is actually less in favor in 1811 than at the beginning of his career. Considers his taste in description to be "childish" and finds no variety in his portrayal of human character. There is little passion except between father and daughter or brothers and sisters, and his picture of society does not extend much beyond that of the privacy of a small family. <u>Kehama</u> is his "most extravagant and elaborate" work with a plot similar to <u>Thalaba</u>. After an exposition of the poem canto by canto, Jeffrey concludes that "it possesses the interest of a fairy tale for children, and not of an Epic poem for men." Complains that "we do not know how to sympathize with persons placed in situations of which we can have no experience." Quotes approvingly, however, the account of the burning of young Arvalan's widow, the pictures of morning and evening, the awaking of Kailyal, and the often-quoted passage "They sin who tell us love can die" (called in the "moralizing style of Walter Scott"). The last ten pages (456-65) of the review quote passages which Jeffrey likes. Concludes with this balanced view of Southey's achievement: "great space we have allowed him to occupy, both now and on former occasions, proves sufficiently what importance we attach to his very errors, and what great things, we think, might be expected from him, if he could only be made to exert himself on the same side with those who have hitherto succeeded in commanding the admiration of the world."

6   SCOTT, WALTER. Review of <u>The Curse of Kehama</u>. <u>Quarterly Review</u>, 5, 40-61.

Summarizes and quotes from the poem stressing the peculiarity of the Hindoo religion and praising the description

of Arvalan's funeral and the curse itself. The poem's "beauties are infinite, and it possesses that high qualification for popularity the power of exciting a painful and sustained interest." The difficult subject has been well handled.
Reprinted 1834.B1.

1813 A BOOKS - NONE

1813 B OTHER WRITINGS

1   ANON. Review of Life of Nelson. British Critic, 43 (October), 360-66.
    Applauds Southey's success in eulogizing Nelson and his discreet treatment of the affair with Lady Hamilton and the government of Naples. "We are, on the whole, exceedingly well pleased with the performance."

2   ANON. Review of Life of Nelson. Critical Review, 4th ser. 4 (July), 11-26.
    Praises Southey's execution of the task, its readable quality, and its impartiality. "Mr. Southey has...a poet's eye and he has ventured to look full and fixedly upon the sunny radiance of Nelson's fame; and has both seen and marked the blots of infirmity, by which it was partially obscured."

1814 A BOOKS -NONE

1814 B OTHER WRITINGS

1   ANON. Review of Carmen Triumphale. Critical Review, 4th ser. 5 (February), 203-08.
    Southey's talents are not suited for writing odes on contemporary events because his whole writing career has been devoted to the "marvellous."

2   ANON. Review of Carmen Triumphale. Eclectic Review, 2nd ser. 1 (April), 431-36.
    Questions whether laureateship should be continued and especially the requirement that odes be written on schedule as part of the official duty. Southey's appointment is the most respectable since Dryden's. Ode praised - especially for the stanza beginning "From Spain the living spark went forth."

1814

3   ANON. Review of <u>Carmen Triumphale</u>. <u>Scourge</u>, 7 (February), 122-30.
    Attacks the change in Southey's early views of society with his new advocacy of the established order. Objects to the style, the irregular stanza, and the "common-place imagery and hackneyed diction."

4   [JEFFREY, FRANCIS (?).] Review of <u>Carmen Triumphale</u>. <u>Edinburgh Review</u>, 22 (January), 447-54.
    "We have always maintained that the writings of Mr. Southey were remarkable, not merely for affectation and bad taste, but for poetical genius of considerable magnitude." Laureate odes, however, should not be published, but since this one has been, it calls for attention. Prints several stanzas from the poem - with some changes - as prose to prove that the poem reads like an extract from a newspaper. Objects to the praise of Spain in the poem because Spain did very little for itself and owes its liberation to British valor and enterprise. The conclusion softens the attack upon Southey: "We think very favourably of his abilities, when his head is clear...We have read his spirited and honest life of Nelson with very great pleasure, and only hesitate about making it the subject of a review, because we believe it to be already almost as popular as it would be our object to make it."

5   ANON. Review of <u>Odes to His Royal Highness the Prince Regent</u>, ...the Emperor of Russia, and...the King of Prussia. <u>British Critic</u>, 2nd ser. 2 (July), 95-98.
    Better than <u>Carmen Triumphale</u>. "We approve highly of the strain of piety which pervades these songs of triumph, it adds a grandeur and dignity to the whole." Southey's laureate style seems based upon Biblical prophetic poetry. Predicts that Southey "will do honour to the laurels which adorn his brow."

1815 A BOOKS - NONE

1815 B OTHER WRITINGS

1   ANON. Review of <u>Roderick</u>. <u>British Review</u>, 6 (November), 287-306.
    Objects to lack of credibility in details of the plot, notably Roderick's successful disguise. The expression of a vindictive spirit seems inconsistent with Roderick's high qualities. The long notes to the poem are protested as a "modern fashion."

1815

2   BEDFORD, GROSVENOR CHARLES. Review of Roderick. Quarterly
    Review, 13 (April), 83-113.
       Admires all aspects of the work. "Original in its plan,
    true in its fundamental elements, and consistent in its
    parts, it rouses the feelings, and stimulates those powers
    of the imagination, which rejoice in the consciousness of
    exertion." Praise for characters of Roderick, Adosinda,
    Count Julian; for the picture of the manners of the Gothic-
    Moorish age; and the contrast between Christians and Mussel-
    men. Commends the versification and declares language of
    the poem as worthy to be "admitted in the mint of Queen
    Elizabeth's Age."

3   COLERIDGE, JOHN TAYLOR. Review of Roderick. British Critic,
    2nd ser. 2 (April), 353-89.
       Southey is "eminently a moral writer; to the high purpose
    implied in this title, the melody of his numbers, the clear
    rapidity of his style, the pathetic power which he exercises
    over our feelings, and the interesting manner of telling his
    story, whether in verse or prose, are all merely contribu-
    tive." Summarizes the plot, praises the character of Rod-
    erick, and asserts that the poem has enough "sword and dag-
    ger" to satisfy any reader.

4   JEFFREY, FRANCIS. Review of Roderick. Edinburgh Review, 25
    (June), 1-31.
       "This is the best, we think, and the most powerful of all
    Mr. Southey's poems. It abounds with lofty sentiments, and
    magnificent imagery; and contains more rich and comprehen-
    sive descriptions - more beautiful pictures of pure affec-
    tion - and more impressive representations of mental agony
    and exaltation than we have often met with in the compass
    of a single volume." Then complains of a style that is
    "too monotonous - too wordy - and too uniformly stately,
    tragical, and emphatic." Its great blemish is the religious
    or fanatical tone. Poem is then summarized, book by book,
    with copious quotations. Concludes that despite "a great
    deal of affectation...the beauties, upon the whole, predom-
    inate; - and these, we hope, speak for themselves in the
    passages we have already extracted." Objects to such words
    as "avid," "aureate," "leman," "frequentage," and "weedery."

5   MERIVALE, JOHN HERMAN. Review of Roderick. Monthly Review,
    n.s. 76 (March), 225-40.
       Despite such faults as being "too long by half, too de-
    clamatory" and too filled with "scriptural phraseology,"
    Roderick will contribute more to Southey's fame than any
    of his previous poems. Praises some beautiful passages but

1815

>
> objects to the prominence given minor characters who have little to do in the plot - such as the young soldier Alphonso and Roderick's mother - and to Southey's efforts to extenuate the fault of his hero.

6   MONTGOMERY, JAMES. Review of Roderick. Eclectic Review, n.s. 3 (April), 352-68.
    Southey fails to conform to the tastes of modern readers; his poems "are addressed to readers, who have either a national antipathy against the burthen of them, as to the dishonour of their country in 'Joan of Arc'; an indifference to super-human exploits and sufferings, as in 'Thalaba'; a horror of barbarity, as to the Mexican scenes of 'Madoc'; a resolute incredulity of monstrous and unclassical mythology, as in 'Kehama'; or an ignorance of the history, and unconcern for the fate of the heroes, as in many instances in 'Roderick,' the last of the Goths." Regrets that the long notes accompanying Southey's poems are necessary. Hopes that he will write a poem from British history on a topic dear to the hearts of his readers. Roderick was historically an infamous character. Objects to a Protestant poet writing a poem addressed to the Virgin Mary (16th section).

1816 A BOOKS - NONE

1816 B OTHER WRITINGS

1   CONDER, JOSIAH. Review of A Poet's Pilgrimage to Waterloo. Eclectic Review, 2nd ser. 6 (August), 1-18.
    An essay-review devoted largely to the difficulties of writing upon contemporary events - and especially war - that are so close to the experience of readers. Southey, however, is best suited of all contemporary authors to treat of such matters, and is commended for the excellence of what he has written: he has thrown no "false glory" on the events of Waterloo. Concludes with a contrast between Wordsworth (his Thanksgiving Ode, January 18, 1816) and Southey in which Wordsworth is compared to "a mountain torrent issuing from some unknown solitude" and Southey to "a mighty stream, eccentric, but clear, rapid, and beautiful, that loves the imaged heavens on its surface and the racy verdure of the earth, and flows and murmurs for man."

2   HAZLITT, WILLIAM. Review of The Lay of the Laureate and Carmen Nuptiale. Examiner, July 7, pp. 426-28.
    Southey's Lay is "beneath criticism" and "a Methodist sermon turned into doggerel verse." Southey's confessed

1817

pride in the office of laureate is unjustified since he is associated with the shortcomings of the Regent. Southey is also accused of feeling superior to the great of the earth - such as Bonaparte - "the true secret of Mr. Southey's excessive anger at the late Usurper."

3   JEFFREY, FRANCIS. Review of The Lay of the Laureate and Carmen Nuptiale. Edinburgh Review, 26 (June), 441-49.
    An attack upon the position of poet-laureate as much as upon the poem: "A Poet-laureate, we take it, is naturally a ridiculous person." The best that he can do is to make himself as inconspicuous as possible. Southey's laureate odes are "utterly and intolerably bad" and far beneath his other works.

1817 A BOOKS - NONE

1817 B OTHER WRITINGS

1   ANON. Review of History of Brazil. Vol. 2. Gentleman's Magazine, 87 (June), 528-29.
    Considers second volume more interesting than the first. Approves of Southey's observation that "the superior prosperity of Brazil" is due "to exemption from the distinction of Casts, which in other European Colonies have uniformly opposed a barrier to the progress of civilization and improvement."

2   ANON. Review of Wat Tyler. Literary Gazette, March 29, pp. 147-48.
    A defense of Southey and an attack upon "the rancorous malevolence or wicked cupidity of those persons who have, contrary to all honour and honesty, sent the poem of Wat Tyler into the world, without the consent of the author."

3   COLERIDGE, SAMUEL TAYLOR. Biographia Literaria; or Biographical Sketches of My Literary Life and Opinions. London: Rest Fenner.
    Chapter three contains Coleridge's tribute to Southey. Coleridge, who attributed some of the attacks upon himself to his intimacy with Wordsworth and Southey, reviews Southey's career emphasizing the severity and unjustness of the attacks upon him. Of his works Coleridge said: "His prose is always intelligible and always entertaining. In poetry he has attempted almost every species of composition known before...and if we except the highest lyric...he has attempted every species successfully." In Roderick Cole-

15

1817

ridge stated that "he has surpassed himself." The chapter concludes with an encomium on Southey's personal worth: "no man was ever a more constant friend, never had poet more friends and honorers among the good of all parties." Reprinted 1907.B1.

4 HAZLITT, WILLIAM. Review of Wat Tyler. Examiner, March 9, pp. 157-59.
Contrasts Wat Tyler with Southey's article on parliamentary reform in the Quarterly for October 1816. The contrast is summed up: "The author of Wat Tyler was an Ultra-jacobin; the author of Parliamentary Reform is an Ultra-royalist; the one was a frantic demagogue; the other is a servile court-fool."

5 HEBER, REGINALD. Review of History of Brazil. Vol. 2. Quarterly Review, 18 (October), 99-128.
Summarizes the Brazilian history in the volume, reserving the highest praise for the account of the Jesuits in Paraguay. Southey has here "most succeeded as an historian. In the account of these strange establishments, his usual minuteness of detail is not only necessary but agreeable and appropriate; while without losing sight of the real faults and follies of these religioners...he has given us such pictures of industry untired, undaunted courage and disinterestedness almost apostolical...as may well kindle the emulation of those who have a purer faith to disseminate." Heber concludes that Southey has devoted too much time to the history of Brazil. Remembering the brilliance of the Life of Nelson he regrets that Southey has been "detained so long, amid the woods and wastes of Paraguay and Pernambuco." Suggests rather such subjects as "the deliverance of Spain by Wellington, and the hurried and eventful scenes of that great drama whose curtain fell at Waterloo."

6 JEFFREY, FRANCIS. Review of Wat Tyler and A Letter to William Smith, Esq. Edinburgh Review, 28 (March), 151-74.
Summarizes and quotes from Wat Tyler and narrates the account of its surreptitious publication twenty-three years after its publication. Its writing is "inconceivably poor and childish....A more pitiful piece of puling indeed was never indited by a young girl at a boarding-school." A young man who wrote in the manner of Wat Tyler at twenty-one is not likely ever to write rationally on political subjects. Jeffrey then summarizes the Letter to William Smith. Southey's complaint that he has been "more attacked and insulted than any man" is answered by the assertion that he

must invite these attacks. "The Antijacobins parodied his Jacobin lyrics and Regicide inscriptions - and the Edinburgh Reviewers made sport with his Laureate odes and his habitual affectations." Concludes by decrying Southey's recommendations in the Quarterly for control of the press, the education of the poor under the direction of the Church of England, and the increase of government expenditure for public works in order to relieve unemployment. The article is thus more an attack upon the Quarterly and the policies of the government than a review of literary works.

1820 A BOOK

1   WATSON, RICHARD. Observations on Southey's 'Life of Wesley.' Being a Defence of the Character, Labours, and Opinions, of Mr. Wesley, Against the Misrepresentations of That Publication. London, 228 pp.
    Despite Southey's diligence in collecting materials, his skill as narrator, and his candor, Watson finds serious objections. Southey judges Wesley by "natural" causes in which devotional feelings are resolved into constitutional habits. When Southey views Wesley and the movement from a Christian point of view it is from that of a member of the Church of England. Watson objects to Southey's comments and reflections on the biography and history of Methodism. Southey was not qualified to judge Wesley's religious character, doctrines, and labors as a minister.

1820 B OTHER WRITINGS

1   HEBER, REGINALD. Review of Life of Wesley. Quarterly Review, 24 (October), 1-55.
    Describes the great extent and growth of Methodism and acknowledges its great good. Thinks Southey is well qualified to give "a sober and impartial estimate of Wesley's character and opinions." His partiality to Wesley has not blinded him to Wesley's love of power. Review retells the life of Wesley, but offers little criticism of Southey's research and writing.

1821 A BOOKS - NONE

1821 B OTHER WRITINGS

1   ANON. Review of A Vision of Judgment. Monthly Review, n.s. 95 (June), 170-78.

1821

Objects not only to the ideas of the poem but to the versification. Analyzes Southey's use of hexameters. Concludes with an "unfeigned depression of such ample powers so uselessly diffused in poetry."

2   JEFFREY, FRANCIS. "Laureate Hexameters." Review of A Vision of Judgment. Edinburgh Review, 35 (July), 422-36.
    This laureate ode "is embodied in the form of a Vision, - which is incredibly absurd and extravagant, without one trait of originality or invention; and, to make it the more gracious, served up in English Hexameters." Hexameters cannot be successful in English measure because English versification depends on accented and unaccented syllables. An English hexameter is "a mass of stiff prose ending in a trivial, lyrical cadence of five swift syllables." Summary of poem includes approbation of the five lines on Southey's native Bristol - the only bit of approval in the review.

1822 A BOOKS - NONE

1822 B OTHER WRITINGS

1   ANON. Review of History of the Peninsular War. Literary Gazette, December 14, pp. 783-84.
    Lauds Southey's achievement. "The matters recorded are worthy of the ablest pen; the style is peculiar, and peculiarly vivid; sometimes highly elevated, always clear and forcible." Southey's indignation in speaking of Bonaparte and Bonaparte's generals in the Peninsula is quite deserved.

1823 A BOOKS - NONE

1823 B OTHER WRITINGS

1   ANON. Review of History of the Peninsular War. Eclectic Review, 2nd ser. 20 (July), 1-22.
    A good subject for which Southey is well qualified. Disappointed, however, in the failure "in detecting the secret motives and springs of action, which is so indispensable a faculty in the historian." In the description of military matters and manoeuvres Southey has "entirely failed." Hopes that future sections of the history "will rouse him into more vigorous narrative."

2   PROCTER, GEORGE and J. W. CROKER. Review of History of the Peninsular War. Quarterly Review, 29 (April), 53-85.

The war itself was a glorious achievement, and Southey was best fitted to record that event. He "has enriched our annals with the first portion of a work which - though not exempt from blemishes - will be found to yield to none of his former prose writings in execution, while it eminently surpasses them all in importance and interest." Southey's volume is summarized by way of retelling the story of the war. Objects to introduction into the text of proclamations, manifestoes, and state papers which could have been abridged. Also objects to insertion of so many stories and legends associated with the places and buildings mentioned in the history.

1824 A BOOKS - NONE

1824 B OTHER WRITINGS

1   ANON. Review of Book of the Church. British Critic. 2nd ser. 21 (May), 449-63.
    A book that was needed, and Southey has planned and executed his work well. "He sketches manners, courts, and systems, with a bold and rapid pencil" and gives "a distinct view of the Church, of its services, and its merits."

2   ANON. Review of Book of the Church. Gentleman's Magazine, 94 (March), 246-48.
    Brief summary with quotations. Observes Southey's "hostility to the Papists" and agrees with him as to the benefits of the Church Establishment to the nation.

3   ANON. "Southey and Byron." Blackwood's Edinburgh Magazine, 16 (December), 711-15.
    Reprints Southey's letter of December 8, 1824 to the Courier defending himself from the charge made by Captain Thomas Medwin in his Conversations that he had spread calumnies against Byron and Shelley and that he was the author of the review of Hunt's Foliage in the Quarterly. Introduction to the reprint stresses the temperamental differences between the two men. "Mr. Southey is, and always was, too much of a monk, to understand a man of the world like Byron; and Byron was too decidedly, or rather too exclusively, a man of the world, to understand a monk like Southey." Concludes that Southey can "rest assured, that no human being ever believed him to be capable of the least of the dirtinesses attributed to him by the drunken imagination of Byron, - or the base and blundering folly of this Captain Medwin."

1824

4   LOCKHART, J. G. Review of Life of Wesley. Blackwood's Edinburgh Magazine, 15 (February), 208-19.
    Surveys Southey's career and concludes that he has had his day - his poems no longer read and his bulky histories - the life of Nelson excepted - vain and ponderous volumes. The subject of Wesley was not suitable for him because he was not a Methodist nor personally acquainted with Wesley. Concludes that fifty pages would tell all that needs to be said about Wesley and the leaders of Methodism.

1825 A BOOKS - NONE

1825 B OTHER WRITINGS

1   ANON. Review of A Tale of Paraguay. Eclectic Review, 42, 328-37.
    Compares the Tale with Campbell's Gertrude of Wyoming, both transatlantic poems. Story of Southey's Tale is "more intense" and "more powerful." Deplores the critical comparison between Campbell and Southey and asserts that posterity will judge "each in his peculiar walk unrivalled." Regrets, however, that Southey ever wrote laureate and political odes and "deserted his proper path."

2   ANON. Review of A Tale of Paraguay. Blackwood's Edinburgh Magazine, 18 (September), 370-77.
    Judges the poem to be "with many paltry, and a few fine passages, an exceedingly poor poem, feeble alike in design and execution." Quotes several hundred lines but with disapproval. Concludes that the Tale is "unworthy of his high genius and reputation."

3   COLERIDGE, JOHN TAYLOR. Review of A Tale of Paraguay. Quarterly Review, 32 (October), 457-67.
    Summarizes the plot with quotations and commends the "clearness of narration," the "idiomatic purity of style," and the "easy flow of versification." The opening dedicatory stanzas of the poem to Southey's daughter are "in their kind among the most exquisite pieces of English poetry." Faults of the poem are the too-long accounts of the habits and customs of the Guarini tribe, the Spanish raids, and the Jesuit missions. Southey also too often moralizes upon an incident. Suggests Southey's purpose is to show us the virtues of faith and gentle virtues - "to make our men bold, honest and affectionate, and our women meek, tender and true."

1829

4   HAZLITT, WILLIAM. "Mr. Southey." The Spirit of the Age.
    424 pp.
        Hazlitt, who first met Southey in 1803 when he was still
    influenced by the dawn of liberty inspired by the French
    Revolution, speaks of him as having "missed his way in
    Utopia" and as "ever in extremes, and ever in the wrong!"
    Of his long epics Hazlitt prefers Joan of Arc "in which the
    love of Liberty is exhaled like the breath of spring."
    Grudgingly grants merit to Southey's writing for the Quar-
    terly because "the spirit of humanity (thanks to Mr. Sou-
    they) is not quite expelled from the Quarterly Review."
    Admires Southey's prose style describing it as "like clear
    sherry with kernels of old authors thrown into it!" and
    commends the translations of the romances, particularly the
    Cid, which he calls a masterpiece. Compares in the final
    paragraph the conversation of Southey and Coleridge - very
    much to the advantage of Coleridge. Hazlitt's picture of
    Southey's personal appearance is of one with "a tall loose
    figure, a peaked austerity of countenance, and no inclina-
    tion to embonpoint, you would say he has something puritani-
    cal, something ascetic in his appearance."
    Reprinted 1930.B2.

5   MILL, JAMES. Review of The Book of the Church. Westminster
    Review, 3 (January), 167+.
        Mill saw in this book a chance to attack the Church of
    England. The book itself Mill called "an old woman's story-
    book; containing tales about the changes of religion, and
    the lives of the workers of wonders in Great Britain."
    Mill objects to calling those who suffered for the Church
    of England saints, since Mill finds the Church not well
    supplied with martyrs and saints. Southey, however, does
    his best with the death scenes of Cranmer, Charles I, Went-
    worth, and Laud. Mill cannot share Southey's high estima-
    tion of Laud for "no human being ever exerted himself more
    strenuously to corrupt the principles of government in any
    country, than did Laud...to strip the people of every secu-
    rity for the righteous administration of their affairs...
    to place his countrymen in the condition of slaves." Mill
    also objects to Southey's misrepresentations of the histo-
    rian Neal, who wrote on the side of the Puritans. The con-
    clusion of the article is an attack upon the Church of En-
    gland and of ecclesiastical establishments in general, a
    view diametrically opposed to Southey's.

1829 A BOOKS - NONE

1829

1829 B OTHER WRITINGS

1   ANON. Review of Colloquies on the Progress and Prospects of Society. Monthly Review, n.s. 119, 382-95.
    Objects to Southey's habit of writing on so many topics, to his failure to distinguish between the speakers of the dialogue, to the lack of that verisimilitude in the dialogue that one finds in Plato's dialogues, to the fact that the ghost does not "preserve the slightest identity with the man called Sir Thomas More," and to the spirit of intolerance, which is its greatest fault. Praises literary quality of the Colloquies, especially the opening, and quotes approvingly a long description of an English November.

2   BLUNT, JOHN JAMES. Review of Colloquies. Quarterly Review, 41 (July), 1-27.
    Describes plan of book and declares it to be "full of wisdom and devotion - of poetry and feeling." Ignores most of the subject matter of the Colloquies, and devotes much space to deploring the low estate of the Church and attributes that condition to the "temper of the times."

3   COLERIDGE, HARTLEY. Review of All for Love and The Pilgrim of Compostella. Blackwood's Edinburgh Magazine, 26 (July), 62-72.
    Opens review with a long introduction on the Roman Catholic faith before summarizing the plot of All for Love. Author is judged to be "in earnest" although Coleridge had at first suspected a "latent irony" in the poem. The Pilgrim, on the other hand, is a comic trifle. Concludes review with a personal tribute to Southey (Hartley Coleridge was a nephew): "We thank him, for giving to the firesides of the public a trifle, originally intended for his own; and glad we are, that after so long a course of arduous and useful labours, pursued through good report and ill report, after trials neither few nor light, and amid meditations that concern the welfare of nations here, and of man hereafter, - he still retains the life and vivacity of his youthful heart, and the merry versatility of his boyish fancy."

1830 A BOOKS - NONE

1830 B OTHER WRITINGS

1   ANON. Review of Colloquies on the Progress and Prospects of Society. Fraser's Magazine, 1 (June), 584-600.

1830

Attacks Macaulay for his review of the Colloquies in the Edinburgh Review. Affirms Southey's influence upon the public and castigates Macaulay for his review. Emphasizes Southey's personal life, sincerity, "earnest wish to further the improvement of his fellow-creatures," and "soundness of his scholarship." Question is asked (but not answered): why should Macaulay have singled out Southey "for his fierce and foul vituperation?"

2 MACAULAY, THOMAS BABINGTON. Review of Colloquies. Edinburgh Review, 50 (January), 528-65.
One of the most famous attacks upon Southey's positions as a critic of society: indeed, Macaulay seems opposed to every thing which Southey supports in the Colloquies. Macaulay contended that after the state had constructed public buildings all further public works such as the construction of canals and railroads should stop. He also opposed state interference in religion and the suppression of publications, and, in opposition to Southey, supported Catholic Emancipation. Macaulay maintains that the manufacturing system and the government's policy of non-interference has lowered prices and brought comforts within the reach of the people beyond any thing those in the age of Thomas More could have imagined. He has only contempt for Southey's description of pleasant cottages for the workers in place of the depressing houses of the manufacturing towns: "Rose-bushes and poor rates, rather than steam-engines and independence." Southey maintained in the Colloquies that the government should take steps to alleviate the condition of the people, to remove the pollution from the air of the manufacturing towns, to provide for education, and to encourage emigration. Macaulay, in opposition, believed that a system of laissez-faire and manufactures would bring about a great new day a century hence (1930). Macaulay stresses Southey's ignorance of economic principles and statistics and his reliance upon taste and feeling: he writes "on sciences of which he has still the very alphabet to learn." The final paragraph reveals Macaulay's fundamental dispute with Southey as he strictly limits the state to "maintaining peace, by defending property, by diminishing the price of law, and by observing strict economy in every department of the state."

3 ST. BARBE, ROGER F. Review of Vindiciae Ecclesiae Anglicanae. Blackwood's Edinburgh Magazine, 27 (March), 465-71.
Book has deserved more attention than it has received

1830

since "a production better suited to disabuse an intelligent mind, hampered in the sophistry, or fascinated by the phantasmagoric illusions of the Romish Church, can hardly be pointed out." Quotes anecdotes and illustrations and commends the short biography of the Venerable Bede. Opening sentence reveals reviewer's sympathy with Southey's point of view: "With all good will to our brethren of the Roman Catholic profession, as individuals, we must look with a wary eye upon them collectedly, as churchmen."

4   SCOTT, WALTER. Review of Southey's edition of The Pilgrim's Progress with a Life of Bunyan. Quarterly Review, 43 (October), 469-94.
    Retells story of Bunyan's life with quotations from Southey's text. Praises the woodcuts (after the pencil of John Martin) of this edition. Offers no sustained criticism of Southey's work but mentions "skill with which Mr. Southey has restored much of Bunyan's masculine and idiomatic English, which had been gradually dropped out of successive impressions by careless, or unfaithful, or what is as bad, conceited correctors of the press." Reprinted 1834.B1.

1831 A BOOKS - NONE

1831 B OTHER WRITINGS

1   LISTER, THOMAS H. Review of John Jones Attempts in Verse... Essay on the Lives and Works of Our Uneducated Poets. By Robert Southey. Edinburgh Review, 54 (August), 69-84.
    Southey's introductory essay gives value to the book. Questions wisdom of publishing Jones's poetry and the implication in Southey's writings that a poor man who writes verses is "more moral than one who discovers a bent for calculation or mechanics." Concludes that "instead of luring them [the uneducated poets] into the flowery region of poetry," [Southey] should "rather teach them to cultivate pursuits which are more in harmony with their daily habits, and to prefer the useful to the ornamental."

2   LOCKHART, JOHN G. Review of John Jones. Attempts in Verse. Quarterly Review, 44 (January), 52-82.
    Offers no critical comment but retells the story of Southey's meeting with Jones in 1827, quotes from Jones's works, and gives accounts of the various "uneducated poets," especially John Taylor "the water poet" to whom eleven pages are devoted.

3   MACAULAY, THOMAS B. Review of The Pilgrim's Progress, with a Life of John Bunyan. Edinburgh Review, 54 (December), 450-61.
    An encomium of Pilgrim's Progress and its universal popularity. The biography, however, cannot add much to Southey's reputation although it is written "in excellent English" and "in excellent spirit." The book itself is "an eminently beautiful and splendid edition." Reprinted 1898.B2.

1834 A BOOKS - NONE

1834 B OTHER WRITINGS

1   LOCKHART, JOHN G. Review of The Doctor. Quarterly Review, 51 (March), 68-96.
    Praises the language, but finds the humor usually ineffective. Tristram Shandy - to which the plan of The Doctor invites comparison - is successful because the "farrago of odd, yet often second-hand learning" in that work is dramatically presented; in The Doctor the same common-place book material is not so presented. Lockhart does not name Southey as the author of this anonymously published work as he had been assured privately that Southey had denied the authorship.

2   SCOTT, SIR WALTER. Miscellaneous Prose Works. Edited by J. G. Lockhart. Edinburgh. 1834-36. 28 vols.
    Scott's reviews of Southey's Cid and his Chatterton are reprinted in volume 17; his reviews of Amadis, Kehama, and Bunyan in volume 18.

1835 A BOOKS - NONE

1835 B OTHER WRITINGS

1   WILSON, JOHN. Review of The Doctor. Blackwood's Edinburgh Magazine, 38 (August), 269-88; (October), 547-72.
    The story of The Doctor is told by copious extracts. Wilson never attributes the work to Southey directly, but he makes himself clear by calling the author one who "studied so earnestly, and understood so clearly, so many salient points in the Progress and Prospects of Society." The essay-review is written in the same discursive style as The Doctor itself.

1836

1836 A BOOKS - NONE

1836 B OTHER WRITINGS

1   MERIVALE, HERMAN. "Recent Lives of Cowper." Review of
    Southey's Works of William Cowper...With a Life of the
    Author. Edinburgh Review, 63 (July), 337-72.
        Reviews Southey's biography and edition with T.S. Grim-
    shawe's edition of William Hayley's biography and Grim-
    shawe's edition of Cowper. Dismisses Grimshawe's edition
    and regrets that publishers' quarrels over copyrighted
    materials prevent either edition from giving the complete
    Cowper correspondence. Compares the charm of Southey's
    style to the same charm in Cowper's letters, but complains
    of Southey's habit of amplifying the biography by inserting
    biographical sketches of the members of Cowper's early
    literary circle. Retells the events of Cowper's life but
    questions the wisdom of Southey's reprinting Cowper's own
    narrative of the events of his insanity on the ground that
    reading such an account might have a dangerous effect upon
    a person whose mind was "not naturally strong."

1839 A BOOKS - NONE

1839 B OTHER WRITINGS

1   DE QUINCEY, THOMAS. "Lake Reminiscences, from 1807 to 1830."
    Tait's Edinburgh Magazine, 6, 453-64; 513-17.
        These well-known reminiscences are better known from
    their republication in Recollections of the Lake Poets
    in the chapters "William Wordsworth and Robert Southey" and
    "Southey, Wordsworth, and Coleridge." De Quincey describes
    Southey's physical appearance, his well-ordered, industrious
    habits, and his library. De Quincey found Southey affable
    and friendly but objected to his reserve and found Words-
    worth a more genial companion.
        Partially reprinted in J. E. Jordan's Everyman's Library
    edition of De Quincey's work (see 1961.A1).

2   MERIVALE, HERMAN. Review of The Poetical Works of Southey,
    collected by himself. Edinburgh Review, 68 (January),
    354-76.
        Considers Southey an example of a poet who draws his mat-
    ter from books and, although such a practice makes him an
    "artificial" writer, he is nonetheless an original one.
    Objects to the lack of variety in his style and ideas.
    Thalaba and Kehama are tales of prodigies with "no descent

26

from the clouds to the earth." Prefers <u>Thalaba</u>: "To our mind, portions of the first seven cantos - particularly the description of the ruins of Babylon, in the fifth - and almost the whole of the last three - are not only the very highest efforts of their author of his serious vein, but hold no mean rank in the English poetry of the present century." Next in rank is <u>Roderick</u>. The "Funeral Song for the Princess Charlotte" is the only laureate ode worth preserving. Southey's true character is found in his ballads, especially those of a comic turn where saints, monks, and devils are the heroes. "There is an odd raciness about these productions which it is impossible to describe, and difficult to compare to any thing else in existence." Closes review by observing the strange fascination which violence and destruction held for Southey evidenced by "the peculiar gusto with which the Saracens are slaughtered all through the twenty books of Don Roderick" and the fascination the "anthropophagous performances of the Indians of Brazil" held for him.

1843 A BOOKS - NONE

1843 B SHORTER WRITINGS

1   LOCKHART, J. G. Review of J. W. Robberds. <u>A Memoir...William Taylor of Norwich</u>. <u>Quarterly Review</u>, 73 (December), 27-68.
    Includes extensive quotations from the Taylor-Southey correspondence with the comment about "the charitable spirit in which he [Southey] tolerated the most flagrant heresies in a friend, with the monastic bitterness of his remarks and reflections concerning real or imagined errors in the conduct or opinions of any person, out of his own <u>set,</u> by whom he conceived the slightest liberty to have been taken with him in his literary capacity." Lockhart strongly disapproved of Taylor, whom he called "the deliberate teacher of pernicious opinions...forwarding some of the most fatal heresies of this age."

2   ROBBERDS, J. W. <u>A Memoir of the Life and Writings of the Late William Taylor of Norwich</u>. London: Murray. Two volumes. I, pp. 523; II, pp. 576.
    Contains not only Southey's letters to Taylor but Taylor's replies. Reflects their wide range of intellectual and literary interests. Taylor and Southey contributed to many of the same periodicals. An important source of primary material for Southey's views on all subjects; information scattered throughout the two volumes.

1844

1844 A BOOKS - NONE

1844 B OTHER WRITINGS

1 ANON. "Southey's Sale and Southey's Poems." Fraser's Magazine, 30, 87-93.
Southey's collection of 14,000 volumes was that of a collector more interested in the contents of books than their outward appearance. His books are complete with few missing leaves and contain his distinctive markings - neat ticks or S's - in the margin. A few books from the collection are described from the sale that lasted sixteen days.

1845 A BOOKS - NONE

1845 B OTHER WRITINGS

1 THOM, J. W., ed. The Life of the Reverend Joseph Blanco White. 3 volumes. London: John Chapman.
Contains twelve letters of Southey to White concerning, for the most part, Spain and Southey's writings against the Roman Catholics. All are found in volume one, passim.

1847 A BOOKS

1 COTTLE, JOSEPH. Reminiscences of Samuel Taylor Coleridge and Robert Southey. London: Houston and Stoneman.
Cottle, early friend and first publisher of Southey, gives an invaluable account of Southey's early days. Cottle prints several letters, but he is not above fabricating one letter from two or three letters. The notes to New Letters (1965.A1) clarify many of Cottle's dubious editorial procedures. Cottle's book is unindexed, but the detailed table of contents provides a quick guide to all topics.

1847 B OTHER WRITINGS - NONE

1848 A BOOKS - NONE

1848 B OTHER WRITINGS

1 CHRISTIE, WILLIAM D. "Coleridge and Southey." A review-article of Joseph Cottle's Reminiscences of Samuel Taylor Coleridge and Robert Southey (1847), the second edition (1847) of S. T. Coleridge's Biographia Literaria, and J. W.

1850

Robberds' Memoir...William Taylor of Norwich (1843).
Edinburgh Review, 87 (April), 368-92.
    The biographies of Coleridge and Southey are yet to be written. "It is impossible to read five pages of Mr. Cottle's reminiscences," Christie observes, "without seeing that he has one of the kindest hearts joined to one of the worst judgments of any man that ever lived." Southey's letters which Cottle publishes do Southey no discredit, but they should not have been published during the lifetime of Coleridge's children when they would "be pained by their uncle's testimony against their father." Southey's life could almost be written from his letters to Taylor - "his letters are the perfection of letter writing, or nearly so; clear, lively, unaffected, largely dashed with humour, and entering into whatever he is writing or reading." Article retells story of the Coleridge-Southey friendship and the scheme of Pantisocracy. Tone of the article is very favorable to Southey without being in the least censorious of Coleridge.

1849 A BOOKS

1   SOUTHEY, C. C. The Life and Correspondences of the Late Robert Southey. London: Longman. Six volumes. 1849-50.
    Contains 741 letters with a running biographical commentary that links the letters. It was reviewed at length in the Quarterly (1850.B1) and the Edinburgh (1851.B1). Its editorial inaccuracies have been frequently indicated (1965.A1).

1849 B SHORTER WRITINGS - NONE

1850 A BOOKS - NONE

1850 B OTHER WRITINGS

1   LANDOR, WALTER SAVAGE. "To the Reverend Charles Cuthbert Southey on His Father's Character and Public Services." Fraser's Magazine, 42, 647-50.
    A laudatory view of Southey's achievement and a regret that the son, for the sake of his father's services to literature and the state, has not received appropriate ecclesiastical preferment. Landor recognized the differences among the three Lake poets: "Southey could grasp great subjects, and completely master them; Coleridge never attempted it; Wordsworth attempted it, and failed." Reprinted 1927.B1.

1850

2   LOCKHART, JOHN GIBSON and WHITWELL ELWIN. Review of C. C.
    Southey's Life and Correspondence of the Late Robert Southey
    (1849-50). Quarterly Review, 88, 197-247.
       Recounts Southey's life stressing his seclusion from many
    of the world's activities and regretting that he had not
    lived a more active life. Southey should not have worked
    and studied so much; he should have spent more time out of
    doors and should have read more for the sheer pleasure of
    reading. The review concludes with a quick survey of Sou-
    they's works. His principal fault in both his prose and
    poetry was prolixity, lack of conciseness, and a fatal ten-
    dency to go into unnecessary detail. Thalaba among the
    long poems is preferred: "the most vigorous, elastic and
    picturesque that ever came from his pen." The letters are
    also especially praised.

1851 A BOOKS - NONE

1851 B OTHER WRITINGS

1   DONNE, WILLIAM BODHAM. Review of C. C. Southey's Life and
    Correspondence of the Late Robert Southey. Edinburgh
    Review, 93 (April), 370-402.
       Surveys Southey's long career as man and writer. Judges
    long poems unsuccessful because Southey's tendency to write
    at length proved damaging to his ultimate poetic achieve-
    ment. Does not totally regret Southey's failure to complete
    his history of the monastic orders, the history of Portugal,
    and the history of English literature because he spent that
    time by writing for the reviews "many beautiful chapters to
    the current consumable literature of his age." Donne ad-
    mires his "clear, masculine, and harmonious style." The
    agreeable accounts of Southey's various trips contained in
    his letters are especially commended. In addition to the
    life of Nelson the lives of Wesley and Cowper should be
    rescued "from the purgatory flames." Biography "compelled
    him to be brief, without denying him the privilege of short
    excursions and legitimate ornament." The Peninsular War is
    judged to be "dead"; the Book of the Church can be read for
    its style if not for its assertions. The Doctor suggests
    that Southey had "powers which, more sedulously cultivated,
    might have enrolled their author in the goodly company of
    British novelists."

1854 A BOOKS

1 BROWNE, C. T. Life of Robert Southey. London: Chapman and Hall.
    A brief summary of the material published in C. C. Southey's Life and Correspondence of the late Robert Southey. Contains a sympathetic account of Southey's interest and encouragement of young literary aspirants and of his loyalty to old friends.

1854 B OTHER WRITINGS - NONE

1856 A BOOKS

1 WARTER, JOHN WOOD, ed. Selections from the Letters of Robert Southey. London.
    This four-volume edition of Southey's correspondence contains several hundred letters with scant annotation but with an index.

1856 B OTHER WRITINGS

1 ANON. "A Quartet of Quarterly Reviewers." Bentley's Miscellany, 40, 320-24.
    Emphasizes the necessity for Southey to review in order to earn his living expenses. "Southey was a jibbing horse in the Quarterly team" and disliked the driver "who had the whip-hand of him, and sometimes touched him on the raw." Nonetheless Southey wrote a "prodigious variety" of articles in "a spirit of industrious research," and with an "unlaboured grace of style." Concludes: "First and last he wrote upon themes so various that they seem to be the epitome of the age, in matters political, economical, and literary."

2 ELWIN, WHITWELL. Review of J. W. Warter's edition of Selections from the Letters of Robert Southey. Quarterly Review, 98 (March), 456-501.
    Objects to Warter's lack of competent editorial skills and to his inclusion of a scriptural parody written by Southey. Gives a biographical sketch of Southey. Devotes several paragraphs to a defense of John Murray, who valued Southey's services and even overpaid him in money for his Quarterly contributions - according to Southey's own testimony. Objects to the practice of editors who publish from private correspondence every opinion of an eminent man: "no censure can be too strong for those who, by printing

1856

>the casual ebullitions of the hour, convert the confidences of intimacy into a public libel upon the dead."

1857 A BOOKS - NONE

1857 B OTHER WRITINGS

1 TUCKERMAN, HENRY T. "Robert Southey, the Man of Letters." Essays, Biographical and Critical. Boston: Philips, Sampson, pp. 59-74.
    Stresses Southey's single-minded devotion to literature and the regularity of his life. Southey's poems are remembered for their fine passages rather than in their entirety. "His great merit as a writer consists in the utility of a portion of his works, and their unexceptionable morality and good sense." Tuckerman also describes Southey as a "verbal architect." But he concludes that Southey lacked the noble and inspired mood that would produce permanent masterpieces. Reprinted as the introduction to the Boston edition of Southey's poetry published in 1860 and frequently reissued thereafter (See 1860.A1).

1858 A BOOKS - NONE

1858 B OTHER WRITINGS

1 DAVY, JOHN, ed. Fragmentary Remains, Literary and Scientific, of Sir Humphry Davy. London: John Churchill, pp. 32-48.
    Davy, the celebrated chemist, was a friend of Southey in Bristol when Davy was the director of the Pneumatic Institute. Southey was interested in Davy's experiments with nitrous oxide (the "laughing gas") and permitted himself to be a subject for experimentation. Davy was also a poet, and Southey published several of his poems in the Annual Anthology (1799).

1860 A BOOKS

1 The Poetical Works of Robert Southey. With a Memoir of the Author. Boston: Little, Brown. Ten volumes.
    [The memoir is by Henry T. Tuckerman (See 1857.B1).]
    This edition includes not only the poems published by Southey in his collected edition of 1837-38 but also the volumes of posthumously published poems. This edition has been reprinted many times - often as ten volumes in five -

by Houghton Mifflin and Company. The edition also includes the prefaces which Southey wrote for each of the ten original volumes (See 1857.B1).

1860 B OTHER WRITINGS

1   THACKERAY, W. M. "The Four Georges." Cornhill Magazine, 2, 385-406.
    A tribute to Southey whom Thackeray describes as "an English worthy" and lauds his life and his letters: "Southey's private letters are worth piles of epics, and are sure to last among us, as long as kind hearts like to sympathize with goodness and purity, and love and upright life." Reprinted in Thackeray's collected works.

1864 A BOOKS - NONE

1864 B OTHER WRITINGS

1   ANON. "Bibliomania." North British Review, 40, 70-92.
    Describes and quotes from Coleridge's copy of the first edition of Joan of Arc (1796). Coleridge's comments are full and frank and are mostly on the language and versification of the poem. Coleridge has also indicated in the margin those parts of Book II which he had written.

1866 A BOOKS - NONE

1866 B OTHER WRITINGS

1   JERDAN, WILLIAM. "Robert Southey." Men I Have Known. London: George Routledge and Sons, pp. 406-20.
    Jerdan records that Southey had little to say in large social groups but was "fluent" only in a circle of two or three companions. Jerdan's sketch of Southey's life is noteworthy for its spirited defense of the second Mrs. Southey.

1869 A BOOKS - NONE

1869 B OTHER WRITINGS

1   FORSTER, JOHN. The Life of Walter Savage Landor. London: Chapman and Hall. Two volumes.
    Contains the bulk of the Southey-Landor correspondence,

1869

>   much of it not available elsewhere. The Southey letters
>   and allusions are scattered throughout the Life.

2   SADLER, THOMAS, ed. The Diary, Reminiscences, and Correspondence of Henry Crabb Robinson. London: Macmillan. Three Volumes.
    Many allusions to Southey in these volumes, which an index makes readily available. Contains three letters by Southey to Robinson and two letters to Elton Hamond. These volumes contain material not included in Edith Morley's edition of Robinson's diaries (See 1938.B3).

1876 A BOOKS - NONE

1876 B OTHER WRITINGS

1   DENNIS, JOHN. "Robert Southey." Studies in English Literature. London: Edward Stanford. New Edition, 1883, pp. 250-87.
    Dennis stresses Southey as an honorable man of letters, who in his personal life was a true friend, accepting the demands of family, friends, and circumstances. Although Dennis cannot praise the epics, he finds Roderick and Kehama the best; he likes the ballads for their comic treatment of melancholy subjects. The failure of so many of Southey's works - notably the History of Brazil - was a failure to estimate the interests of the public. Dennis finds Southey's social criticism in his essays and letters far ahead of his time. But Dennis is especially censorious about the deficiencies of Cuthbert Southey's Life and Correspondence and the injudicious editing of Warter's edition of the Letters.

1879 A BOOKS

1   DOWDEN, EDWARD. Southey. English Men of Letters Series. London.
    Dowden's portrait of Southey softens the harsh side of his personality and presents him as happy in his family and friends, deeply engrossed in the writing of his books and articles. The account is chronological for the first thirty years, but then becomes a series of sketches of various incidents, friendships, and literary projects. Dowden is brief on the friendships with Coleridge and Wordsworth, but he is good for his recognition of the importance of Epictetus in Southey's development, his picture of the William Taylor group at Norwich, his description of Greta

Hall and the Lake District, the enthusiasm of Southey for books and the creation of his library. Highest praise is reserved for Southey's biographies; in his poetry Dowden emphasizes the "high-souled" and moral qualities of his dedicated heroes and heroines. Dowden's partiality for Southey results in a portrait that is almost saintly.

1879 B OTHER WRITINGS - NONE

1881 A BOOKS

1   DOWDEN, EDWARD, ed. The Correspondence of Southey with Caroline Bowles: To Which Are Added Correspondence with Shelley, and Southey's Dreams. Dublin: Hodges, Figgis; London: Longman, 388 pp.
    Contains a long and sympathetic introduction describing Southey's friendship with Caroline Bowles which culminated in their marriage in 1839. The letters to and from Shelley appeared in this volume for the first time.

1881 B OTHER WRITINGS

1   CARLYLE, THOMAS. Reminiscences. Edited by J. A. Froude. London: Longman.
    Carlyle in 1867 recorded his association with Southey which had begun, first, by a reading of his poems, his Quarterly articles, and secondly through a series of meetings arranged by Henry Taylor (1835-38). Carlyle's description of Southey's physical appearance - often quoted - is vivid and detailed. Southey praised Carlyle's French Revolution: "My poor French Revolution evidently appeared to him a Good Deed." Carlyle and Southey talked of moral and social topics, not literature; Southey was the first man of literary eminence to praise Carlyle's work.

1887 A BOOKS

1   DENNIS, JOHN, ed. Robert Southey: The Story of His Life Written in His Letters. Boston: Lothrop; reprinted in 1894 in Bohn's Standard Library.
    A selection of Southey's published letters arranged so as to narrate his biography.

1887 B OTHER WRITINGS

1   KNIGHT, W., ed. Memorials of Coleorton: Being Letters from

1887

Coleridge, Wordsworth and His Sister, Southey and Sir Walter Scott, to Sir George and Lady Beaumont 1803-34. Edinburgh: D. Douglas. Two volumes. I, 227 pp.; II, 294 pp.
Southey's letters to the well-known patron of arts and letters are scattered throughout the second volume.

1889 A BOOKS - NONE

1889 B OTHER WRITINGS

1   COLERIDGE, E. H., ed. Letters from the Lake Poets to Daniel Stuart. London: Privately printed, pp. 387-434.
Contains Southey's letters to Stuart, editor of the Morning Post, and some poems intended as contributions to the Post.

1891 A BOOKS - NONE

1891 B OTHER WRITINGS

1   SMILES, SAMUEL. A Publisher and His Friends: Memoir of the Late John Murray. London: Murray; New York: Scribner's. Two volumes, I, 496 pp.; II, 549 pp., passim.
Contains many extracts from letters of Southey to Murray about the books of Southey which Murray published and of his articles for the Quarterly. An index facilitates finding the scattered Southey material.

1895 A BOOKS

1   HANNAY, DAVID, ed. English Seamen. London: Methuen.
A reprint of Southey's naval biographies from Lives of the British Admirals (1833). These short biographies are of Sir Richard Hawkins, Sir Richard Grenville, Robert Devereux, Second Earl of Essex, and Sir Walter Raleigh.

1895 B OTHER WRITINGS

1   SAINTSBURY, GEORGE. "Robert Southey." Essays in English Literature, Series Two. London: Dent; New York: Scribner's, pp. 1-37.
Recounts Southey's career and comments briefly upon all his works. Saintsbury points out the inaccuracy of the charge that Southey was a "Mr. Feathernest" by stressing how small were the financial rewards of his writing. Of

the poems, preference is given to <u>Roderick</u> and <u>Kehama</u>, the latter of which receives a detailed analysis. Saintsbury's conclusion is that only a reader who has "worked through the enormous mass of his verse, his prose, and his letters can fully appreciate his merits." An Appendix "Coleridge and Southey" (pp. 415-17) defends Southey against the charge (made by J. D. Campbell in his biography of Coleridge) that Southey forced Coleridge to marry Sara Fricker. Southey could not have foreseen the outcome of the marriage nor sensed Coleridge's instability of temperament, (See 1923.B2).

1897 A BOOKS - NONE

1897 B OTHER WRITINGS

1   DOWDEN, EDWARD. "Early Revolutionary Group and Antagonists." <u>The French Revolution and English Literature</u>. London: Kegan Paul; New York: Scribner's, pp. 141-93.
    Chapter includes a survey of most of Southey's early poetry with the conclusion that his revolutionary ardor was "more of the heart than of the understanding." It was the humanitarian complexion of the Revolution that appealed to him, and when his hopes for the Revolution failed, he did not cease in his later writings - the <u>Colloquies</u> - to plead for the cause of reformation in society.

1898 A BOOKS - NONE

1898 B OTHER WRITINGS

1   HERAUD, EDITH. <u>Memoirs of John A. Heraud</u>. London: G. Redway.
    Contains Southey's letters to Heraud, poet and <u>Quarterly</u> reviewer. Perhaps the most interesting bit in these letters is the evidence that Southey had read Keats's poetry: "Keats buries himself in the exuberance of his ornaments" - so Southey commented on January 30, 1821.

2   <u>The Complete Works of Lord Macaulay</u>. London: Longmans Green.
    Reprints Macaulay's review of Southey's <u>Colloquies</u>, 8, 450-502; and his review of Bunyan, 7, 605-21.

1899 A BOOKS - NONE

1899

1899 B OTHER WRITINGS

1   FESTING, GABRIELLE. "Literary Friendships: Coleridge and
    Southey." John Hookham Frere and His Friends. London:
    James Nisbet, pp. 217-34.
      Contains Southey's letters to Frere and an account of
    their relationship: Frere often helped Southey in his
    Spanish and Portuguese studies supplying him with materials.

1902 A BOOKS

1   NICOLL, W. ROBERTSON, ed. Journal of a Tour in the Netherlands
    in the Autumn of 1815. Boston: Houghton Mifflin; London:
    W. Heinemann, 1903.
      First publication of Southey's journal of his trip to
    Waterloo and the Low Countries with a short introduction
    and notes by the editor. A Dutch translation appeared in
    1946.

1902 B OTHER WRITINGS

1   SCOTT, HAROLD SPENCER. "Some Southey Letters." Atlantic
    Monthly, 89, 36-45.
      Extracts from 27 letters to Mary Barker, whom Southey
    first met in Portugal in 1796, and who later lived as a
    neighbor in Keswick.

2   STEPHEN, LESLIE. "Southey's Letters." Studies of a Biographer.
    London: Duckworth and Company, IV, 42-79.
      Although Stephen cannot admit Southey to the highest group
    of authors, he can enjoy the ballads; in the quarrel with
    Macaulay he feels Southey to have had the best of the argu-
    ment; and he calls "The Story of the Three Bears" Southey's
    masterpiece. His praise of the letters is qualified on the
    ground that readers of letters enjoy those by authors with
    less stoical reserve than Southey.

1905 A BOOKS - NONE

1905 B OTHER WRITINGS

1   BETHAM, ERNEST. A House of Letters. London: Jarrold, 291 pp.,
    passim.
      Contains letters by Southey to Mary Matilda Betham, author
    and miniaturist, with an account of her friendship with Sou-
    they, Coleridge, and Lamb.

1909

2   CESTRE, CHARLES. La Révolution francaise et les poètes anglais (1789-1809). Dijon: Barbier-Marilier; Paris: Hachette, 1906, 556 pp.
    This monograph is devoted to Wordsworth, Coleridge, and Southey. Cestre surveys Southey's early life, his meeting with Coleridge, the development of pantisocracy - the basis of which he finds in Godwin's philosophy - and then discusses the early poems. A detailed discussion of Wat Tyler and Joan of Arc emphasizes Southey's sympathy for the people as they suffer under their powerful oppressors. Cestre finds Southey's revolutionary enthusiasm much weaker than that of Wordsworth and Coleridge. Southey was not a deep thinker - like Coleridge - and in his revolutionary enthusiasm he was responding to the current sentiment of the times and following late eighteenth-century literary attitudes. Southey does not appear to advantage in his revolutionary poems because he was not at home in revolutionary speculations. The trip to Portugal in 1795-96 marked the end of his radical commitment as he turned to an ideal of a quiet domestic life devoted to poetry and writing.

3   DICEY, A. V. "The Growth of Collectivism." Lectures on the Relation Between Law and Public Opinion in England During the Nineteenth Century. London: Macmillan, 506 pp.
    Dicey observes that Southey, Carlyle, and Dr. Arnold all objected to the dominant individualism of the age. "... while Southey's literary reputation has declined, his ideas on social questions exerted a permanent influence." Dicey concludes that Southey "is to us the prophetic precursor of modern collectivism."

1907 A BOOKS - NONE

1907 B OTHER WRITINGS

1   COLERIDGE, S. T. Biographia Literaria. Edited by J. Shawcross. Two volumes. Oxford: Clarendon Press. Chapter III, 1, 34-49.
    Reprint of 1817.B1.

1909 A BOOKS

1   FITZGERALD, M. H., ed. Poems of Robert Southey Containing Thalaba, The Curse of Kehama, Roderick, Madoc, A Tale of Paraguay, and Selected Minor Poems. London: Henry Frowde, Oxford University Press.

1909

A one-volume selection of Southey's poetry with excellent notes and a bibliography listing the poems not included. Does not include Joan of Arc, but does include the prefaces which Southey wrote for the collected edition of his poetry in 1837-38. There is also a Biographical Table of Southey's life and a short List of Authorities.

1909 B OTHER WRITINGS

1   SYMONS, ARTHUR. "Robert Southey (1774-1843)," The Romantic Movement in English Poetry. London: Constable; New York: Dutton, pp. 148-60.
    Symons finds little to praise in Southey's works because he "had no new vision of the world; he came with no new music." He was not a good critic of literature because he confused virtue with genius. As a man Southey is irritating because of his "conscious rectitude." His prose, if faultless, has only negative merits and is "without magic." Symons cannot admire Southey's experiments in rhymeless verse copied from Sayers. His long poems might as well have been written in prose - even Roderick, the best, Symons avers, of the group. The one section of Southey's achievement which Symons can admire is the group of short poems dealing with the grotesque and showing an ironical humor, of which the finest is "The Battle of Blenheim." Symons' conclusion is that Southey's "talent was pedestrian, and it was his misfortune that he tried to fly."

1911 A BOOKS

1   BUTLER, H. B., ed. The Life of Nelson. London: Henry Frowde, Oxford University Press.
    Introduction and notes with an appendix, "The Nelson Touch."

1911 B OTHER WRITINGS

1   WILLIAMS, ORLO. Lamb's Friend the Census-Taker: Life and Letters of John Rickman. London: Constable; Boston: Houghton Mifflin (1912), 330 pp., passim.
    Southey figures prominently in this biography of one of his best friends, John Rickman, the secretary to the speaker of the House of Commons. Rickman sent Southey material on the poor laws and economics for his books and reviews. Rickman and Southey planned and virtually completed a sequel to Southey's Colloquies. This book contains not only many of Rickman's letters to Southey, but Southey's replies.

Rickman accompanied Southey on his tours to Scotland and the Netherlands, and Rickman's London house was often Southey's home on his visits to London.

1912 A BOOKS

1   FITZGERALD, M. H., ed. <u>Letters of Southey: A Selection</u>. World's Classics Series. Oxford: Oxford University Press.
    A one-volume selection of Southey's letters largely, but not exclusively, derived from C. C. Southey's and J. W. Warter's editions of the correspondence. The introduction is both informative and appreciative, and the notes, although rather brief, are helpful.

1912 B OTHER WRITINGS

1   ELTON, OLIVER. "Southey and Landor." <u>A Survey of English Literature, 1780-1830</u>. London: E. Arnold. Two volumes, II, 1-12.
    A sympathetic account of Southey's career with the conclusion that Southey "if not in any strict sense a great writer, is often, nay, is instinctively, a sound and a good one...and he left the status of men of letters...higher than he found it."

1913 A BOOKS

1   GRANNIS, RUTH S. <u>An American Friend of Southey (Maria Gowen Brooks)</u>. Privately printed.
    Mrs. Brooks (1794-1845) corresponded with Southey and stayed for several weeks at Keswick in 1831. Southey supervised the publication in London of her <u>Zophiel</u> and published an excerpt from that poem in chapter 54 of <u>The Doctor</u>. Mrs. Brooks used the pseudonym "Maria del Occidente" (See 1926.B3).

1913 B OTHER WRITINGS

1   PFANDL, LUDWIG. "Southey und Spanien." <u>Revue Hispanique</u>, 28, 1-315.
    This thorough study (written in German) includes Portugal within its compass and is a comprehensive treatment of all Southey's personal, literary, and historical connections with the Peninsula. Pfandl sees in Southey a pioneer in these studies, but one who lacked the insight into the connections of Portuguese-Spanish literature with its continen-

1913

tal models. Southey's personal impressions of Spain and Portugal are compared with those of other travelers, and an excellent map shows all the places Southey visited. Pfandl censures Southey's translation of Amadis of Gaul for eliminating the love scenes in favor of the marvelous adventures. In Southey's translation of the Cid and his revision of Anthony Munday's translation of Palmerin of England Pfandl objects to Southey's use of Biblical English. Much of Pfandl's work is devoted to a study of Southey's sources. Pfandl concludes his study by discussing the historical materials of Roderick, The Pilgrim of Compostella, and ballads based upon Spanish subjects. Every thing that concerns Spain and Portugal in Southey's work is discussed somewhere in this monograph.

1914 A BOOKS - NONE

1914 B OTHER WRITINGS

1   SAINTSBURY, GEORGE. "Southey. Lesser Poets of the Later Eighteenth Century." Cambridge History of English Literature. Cambridge: Cambridge University Press, 11, 153-71.
    A survey of Southey's life and works with at least a sentence or two of comment on all the works. Saintsbury praises the ballads and devotes an entire page to The Doctor. "Therefore, whatever may be his shortcomings, or, to put it more exactly, his want of supremacy, it must be a strangely limited history of English literature in which a high position is not allowed to Southey."

1915 A BOOKS - NONE

1915 B OTHER WRITINGS

1   LOUNSBURY, T. R. "Southey as Poet and Historian." YR, new series, 4, 330-51.
    Condemns Southey for his bitter and uncharitable remarks, for his bigotry, and for too much confidence in the rightness of his own point of view. Southey was too partisan to be a good historian, and his ideas of historical research were "elementary."

1916 A BOOKS

1   ZEITLIN, JACOB, ed. Select Prose of Robert Southey. New York: Macmillan.

1918

The only anthology devoted to a selection of Southey's voluminous prose publications. Includes a description of Southey's library (Colloquies); scenes from the Lake District (Espriella, Common-Place Book, Colloquies); 200 pages of The Doctor; the life of Bayard (Quarterly, 1825); the siege of Zaragoza and the uprising at Marvam (Peninsular War); the system of the Jesuits in Paraguay (History of Brazil); the manufacturing system (Espriella). Contains an introduction and notes to the selections.

1917 A BOOKS

1   HALLER, WILLIAM. The Early Life of Robert Southey 1774-1803. New York: Columbia University Press, 300 pp.
    This biographical and critical monograph is a thorough account of Southey's early career. The critical emphasis is literary, showing the relationship of Southey's poetry to his eighteenth-century models and to the same literary currents that produced Wordsworth's Lyrical Ballads. Haller sees Southey's strong desire for a home and the opportunity for a life of learned leisure as the determining force in the decade prior to his final settlement at Greta Hall in Keswick. Haller calls attention to the importance of Charles Lamb and his correspondence to both men and carefully discusses the quarrel with Coleridge over the ending of the pantisocratic dream without blaming either one. Haller comments on all the poems of this period, and his accounts of Joan of Arc and Thalaba are the fullest in print. Joan owed its popularity to its political sympathy for the French Revolution and its use of the contemporary interest in a Rousseauistic natural religion. Haller would call Southey's Joan of Arc a Mary Wollstonecraft in armor rather than to use Coleridge's phrase of Joan as "a Tom Paine in petticoats." Haller's account of Thalaba considers its sources, stresses its pioneering use of Oriental materials, but concludes that the poem does not give a lifelike sense of the place and times. But still he finds "the performance so near to success that the reader is surprised to find the poem more beautiful than he had expected or remembered."

1917 B OTHER WRITINGS - NONE

1918 A BOOKS - NONE

1918

1918 B OTHER WRITINGS

1   ZEITLIN, JACOB. "Southey's Contributions to the Critical Review. N & Q, 136 (February-May), 35-36, 66-67, 94-96, 122-24.
    A discussion, identification, and listing of Southey's reviews for the Critical Review for 1798 to 1803. Zeitlin lists twenty-four reviews which he can attribute to Southey with some confidence based upon the evidence of Southey's letters and upon internal evidence derived from a similarity of Southey's views and ideas expressed in his letters and other writings.

1919 A BOOKS - NONE

1919 B OTHER WRITINGS

1   BEER, MAX. A History of British Socialism. London: Allen and Unwin. Reprinted 1940.
    Southey, more than Wordsworth or Coleridge, had the most anti-capitalistic spirit; Beer calls him "one of the keenest and most one-sided critics of the industrial revolution." (Part II, Chapter 9 "Social Conservative Critics - Southey's Prospects of Society," pp. 275-79.)

2   BUCETA, ERASMO. "Two Spanish Ballads Translated by Southey." MLN, 34, 329-36.
    Publishes two unpublished translations by Southey from the Spanish, "Abenamar, Abenamar," and "The Funeral of Aliator." Manuscripts in the Ticknor Collection, Boston Public Library.

1921 A BOOKS - NONE

1921 B OTHER WRITINGS

1   BROADUS, E. K. The Laureateship: A Study of the Office of Poet Laureate in England. Oxford: Clarendon Press, pp. 163-82.
    Southey's laureateship marks the beginning of the modern conception of the office. "Southey was a man of firm character and honest convictions, and he gave expression to his convictions in his laureate verse with a vigour which quite transcended the traditional limitations of the laureateship. Throughout all his odes run two unfailing strains - deep Christian faith and a profound concern for the moral and political welfare of his country."

Robert Southey: A Reference Guide

1923

1922 A BOOKS

1   CALLENDER, GEOFFREY, ed. The Life of Nelson. London: Dent; New York: Dutton.
    Contains a lengthy introduction, notes, and maps of the several naval battles in which Nelson was engaged. Callender, an expert in naval affairs and naval history, points out several errors Southey made. This edition is the fullest and most elaborate of the various editions of Southey's Life of Nelson. The appendix provides a series of questions on the contents of each chapter.

1922 B OTHER WRITINGS

1   BUCETA, ERASMO. "Una Traducción de Lope de Vega Hecha por Southey." RR, 13, 80-83.
    This translation, "The Madonna's Lullaby," was not included in Southey's collected poetical works.

2   HALLER, WILLIAM. "Southey's Later Radicalism." PMLA, 37, 281-92.
    A summary of the evidence provided by Southey's Colloquies (1829) and Essays (1832) for his criticism of society and his suggestions for its improvement. Haller traces these views back to Godwin, especially the view that the individual will act in the best interests of society. Southey's "true strength was perceived by Carlyle," and his praise of Southey's Quarterly articles is cited to counteract the view that derives from Byron and Macaulay.

1923 A BOOKS - NONE

1923 B OTHER WRITINGS

1   GRAHAM, WALTER. "Robert Southey as Tory Reviewer." PQ, 2, 97-111.
    This essay seems to answer Haller's PMLA article (1922.B2) stressing that although Southey is "Humanitarian in everything else, in domestic politics he became an unfeeling obstructionist when the Church and the Constitution seemed to be threatened." Graham's conclusion is that "for thirty years Southey was the intolerant champion and abettor of a group of Ultra-Tories."

2   SAINTSBURY, GEORGE. Collected Essays and Papers. London: Dent, I, 239-67; 267-68.
    Reprints essays "Robert Southey" and "Coleridge and Southey" from Essays in English Literature (See 1895.B1).

1924

1924 A BOOKS - NONE

1924 B OTHER WRITINGS

1   KAUFMAN, PAUL. "The Reading of Southey and Coleridge: The Record of Their Borrowings from the Bristol Library 1793-8." MP, 21, 317-20.
    A list of books borrowed by Southey and Coleridge. A fuller listing will be found in Whalley's article in RES (1950.B3).

1925 A BOOKS

1   CHILDERS, J. S., ed. The Lives and Works of the Uneducated Poets. London: Milford.
    A reprint of Southey's introduction to Attempts in Verse by Jones (1831, 1836), which contained an essay on the lives and works of uneducated poets. The editor provides a brief introduction and notes.

2   FITZGERALD, M. H., ed. The Life of Wesley. London: Oxford University Press.
    This reprint of Southey's Wesley includes the copious notes of Coleridge (published in the third edition). The editor provides an introduction and notes.

1925 B OTHER WRITINGS

1   CHAMBERS, R. W. "Ruskin (and Others) on Byron." English Association Pamphlet, No. 62, 28 pp.
    Defends Southey from charges originating from Byron, Shelley, and their defenders by asking the question: "...should respect for Byron and Shelley involve our thinking of Coleridge and Southey, under the Castlereagh administration, as an 'opium-eater' and a 'renegade' under the administration of a 'jackal'?"
    Reprinted in Chambers's Man's Unconquerable Mind (See 1939.B1).

1926 A BOOKS - NONE

1926 B OTHER WRITINGS

1   BRINTON, CRANE. "The First Generation of Revolt." Political Ideas of the English Romanticists. London: Humphry Milford, Oxford University Press, pp. 48-107.
    Admires Southey's character: "His frank acceptance of life, his dislike of systems, his common sense, always at

the mercy of his enthusiasms but never the dupe of introspection, happily complement the other-worldliness of Coleridge and the self-searching intensity of Wordsworth." Brinton explains thus Southey's seeming inconsistency: "If Southey seems an inconsistent politician he is always a consistent humanitarian."

2   GREEVER, GARLAND. A Wiltshire Parson and His Friends. Boston: Houghton Mifflin, pp. 37-71.
    Prints the letters of Southey to William Lisle Bowles and Bowles's letters to Caroline Bowles.

3   MABBOTT, T. O. "Newly Identified Lines by Southey." N & Q, 151 (July 10), 26.
    The second quatrain of the second canto of Zophiel (1833) by Maria Gowen Brooks ("Maria del Occidente") is presumably by Southey. Lines are quoted (See 1913.A1).

1927 A BOOKS - NONE

1927 B OTHER WRITINGS

1   LANDOR, WALTER SAVAGE. Complete Works. Edited by T. Earle Welby and Stephen Wheeler. London: Chapman and Hall. 16 volumes. 1927-36.
    Reprints Landor's "Open Letter to Charles Cuthbert Southey" (See 1850.B1), 12, 154-60.

2   MORLEY, EDITH J., ed. The Correspondence of Henry Crabb Robinson with the Wordsworth Circle 1808-1866. Oxford: Clarendon Press. Two Volumes.
    Many passing references to Southey and his family - but relatively few to his works - by Robinson and members of the Wordsworth family. Contains many references to the Southey family following the poet's death in 1843.

3   PECK, WALTER E. Shelley: His Life and Work. Boston: Houghton Mifflin. Two Volumes.
    Interchapters on Shelley's sources list many parallels between Shelley's poems and Southey's.

4   WALTER, FÉLIX. "Autour de Southey (1796-1808)." La littérature portugaise en Angleterre a l'époque romantique. Paris: Champion, pp. 56-80.
    A review of Southey's travels in Portugal, his Portuguese studies, and his works touching on that country. Southey is viewed in relation to other contemporary writers on Por-

tuguese subjects (Strangford and Bowles). German scholars, it is noted, had begun to study Portuguese literature and history, but Southey remains as the outstanding British figure of Anglo-Portuguese studies.

1928 A BOOKS - NONE

1928 B OTHER WRITINGS

1   DAVIS, BERTRAM R. "Coleridge and the 'Forty Youths of Bristol.'" TLS, October 11, p. 759.
    Quotes a description of Southey written about 1794 from a Bristol pamphlet, The Observer. Reprinted in New Letters, I, 42n.

2   FAIRCHILD, H. N. "Wordsworth, Southey, and Coleridge." The Noble Savage. New York: Columbia University Press, pp. 172-228.
    Southey's interest in savage life was enduring as is shown in his poems on the slave trade, his "Botany-Bay Eclogues," and especially in Madoc, a poem "crammed with savage lore." In later years Southey's reviews of travellers among primitive peoples reveal his continuing interest in savage life. The conclusion, however, is that "the more Southey knows about the real savage the less he believes in the Noble Savage."

3   KNOWLTON, E. C. "Southey's Eclogues." PQ, 7, 231-41.
    Surveys Southey's four "Botany-Bay Eclogues" and his five English Eclogues stressing their humanitarian and often realistic points of view and suggesting that Southey "had in mind a new sort of pastoral romance." The old classical form was gone. "...the eclogues of Southey signified a dissolution of the classical form in another way and, in substitution for it, a groping toward the dramatic monologue as the nineteenth century came to realize it."

1929 A BOOKS

1   HERFORD, C. H., ed. Journal of a Tour in Scotland in 1819. London: Murray.
    Southey made his Scottish tour (August 17 to October 1) in the company of John Rickman and Thomas Telford, the engineer who had designed many roads, bridges, and the famous Caledonian Canal. Rickman and Telford were on an official trip of inspection, and this circumstance - together with

the professional knowledge of his companions - gave Southey opportunities for seeing and understanding much more than would have been possible for the mere tourist.

1929 B OTHER WRITINGS

1 COBBAN, ALFRED. Edmund Burke and the Revolt Against the Eighteenth Century: A Study of the Political and Social Thinking of Burke, Wordsworth, Coleridge and Southey. London: Allen and Unwin, 280 pp.
   Cobban is impressed by Southey's awareness of the loss a nation suffers by a sole concern with the acquisition of wealth. As early as 1812 Southey had a vision of the British Commonwealth of Nations and had abandoned the old idea of colonies as existing only for the benefit of the mother country.

2 HAVENS, R. D. "A Project of Wordsworth's." RES, 5, 320-22.
   A Southey letter of October 19, 1808 (later published New Letters, I, 483-85) makes clear the involvement of Southey, Wordsworth, Spedding, and Calvert in a move to protest the Convention of Cintra.

3 KNOWLTON, E. C. "Southey's Monodramas." PQ, 8, 408-10.
   Southey's seven monodramas (1793-1802) in blank verse show him "feeling his way toward what was called by Browning 'dramatic lyric' or 'dramatic idyl.'"

4 RICHTER, HELENE. "Robert Southey." Anglia, 53, 288-334, 440-64.
   A narrative of Southey's life and an account of his works arranged by category and by chronology.

1930 A BOOKS

1 FITZGERALD, M. H., ed. The Doctor. London: Bell.
   This abridgement with its introduction and annotation is the most recent reprint of The Doctor. The abridgement permits the slender narrative of Dr. Daniel Dove and his affairs to stand out more clearly than in the seven-volume original, where the many digressions often forget the plot.

1930 B OTHER WRITINGS

1 FEILING, KEITH. "Southey and Wordsworth." Sketches in Nineteenth Century Biography. London and New York: Longmans, Green, pp. 71-84.

1930

        Reviews Southey's career and praises his patriotism and his concern for the quality of human life. "No man better illustrates the reality of that never-yet wholly severed link between one sort of Tory and one sort of Socialist."

2   HAZLITT, WILLIAM. <u>The Complete Works</u>. Edited by P. P. Howe. 21 volumes. London: Dent.
      This standard edition of Hazlitt's works collects and reprints all of Hazlitt's reviews and references to Southey. The full index in the last volume makes the material easily accessible.
    Reprints 1816.B2 in 7, 85-97; 1817.B3 in 7, 168-76; 1825.B1 in 11, 78-86.

3   LOGAN, Sister EUGENIA. "Coleridge's Scheme of Pantisocracy and American Travel Accounts." <u>PMLA</u>, 45, 1069-84.
      Shows the connection between pantisocracy and the efforts of various promoters to encourage emigration to the United States.

4   MEYERSTEIN, E. H. W. <u>A Life of Thomas Chatterton</u>. London: Ingpen and Grant; New York: Scribner's, pp. 491-97, 525-26.
      Contains an account of the circumstances leading to the publication of Cottle's and Southey's edition of Chatterton's <u>Works</u> (1803) for the benefit of Chatterton's mother and sisters. Also prints a letter of Southey's declining to write an epitaph for a proposed monument to Chatterton.

5   PARTINGTON, WILFRED, ed. <u>The Private Letter-Books of Sir Walter Scott</u>. London: Hodder and Stoughton, pp. 72-84.
      The chapter, "The Troubles and Triumphs of Poets," contains extracts from several of Southey's letters to Scott.

<u>1931 A BOOKS - NONE</u>

<u>1931 B OTHER WRITINGS</u>

1   FAIRCHILD, H. N. "The Pantisocratic Phase." <u>The Romantic Quest</u>. New York: Columbia University Press, pp. 50-69.
      Recounts the story of the meeting of Coleridge and Southey and their development of the scheme of pantisocracy. Fairchild stresses the Godwinian strain in pantisocracy as "the application of Godwin's idea of perfectibility through reason to a selected group of people in an environment that had the negative advantage of shutting out opportunities for evil."

1932

2 MacGILLIVRAY, J. R. "The Pantisocracy Scheme and Its Immediate Background." Studies in English by Members of University College. Toronto: University of Toronto Press, pp. 131-69.
    The pantisocrats could have gleaned details of life in America from works by J. P. Brissot, Thomas Cooper, Dr. Joseph Priestley. Brissot's description of central Pennsylvania was very complimentary, and it was in this area that Priestley and Cooper sought settlers. Priestley himself emigrated and lived near the forks of the Susquehannah until his death in 1804.

1932 A BOOKS

1 ROBERTS, R. ELLIS, ed. A Vision of Judgment (with Byron's Vision of Judgement). Harrow Weald: R. A. Maynard and H. W. Bray.
    Introduction sets forth the circumstances of the composition and publication of the two poems.

1932 B OTHER WRITINGS

1 GRIGGS, E. L. "Southey and the Edinburgh Review," MP, 30, 100-103.
    Prints letter of Southey to Coleridge (December 9, 1807) in which Southey declines to write for the Edinburgh because of its literary creed (its blindness to Wordsworth's merits) and its political and moral philosophy.

2 HAVENS, R. D. "Southey's Contributions to the Foreign Review." RES, 8, 210-11.
    Southey wrote four reviews for the Foreign Review and one for the Foreign Quarterly Review.

3 MARCUS, H. "Underdrückte Revolutionsverse des jungen R. Southey." Archiv, 161, 44-51; 173-90.
    Discussion of the trial and conviction of Thomas Muir and Thomas Palmer and the revolutionary background of the 1790's. The article reprints the poem, "The Exiled Patriots," from Galignani's unauthorized collection of Southey's poetry published in Paris in 1829. (The poem was first printed in 1795 in Coleridge's A Moral and Political Lecture.) Southey did not include the poem in his collected edition of 1837-38.

4 WRIGHT, H. G. "Southey's Relations with Finland and Scandinavia." MLR, 27, 149-67.
    "The survey of Southey's relations with Scandinavia and Finland shows how an early interest was revived and fortified in the twenties and thirties; it illustrates his wide

1932

reading, his eagerness in the pursuit of curious lore, and the fertility of his mind in forming literary projects, it bears witness to his love of peace and his hatred of oppression." Southey also reviewed travels to those countries and so much admired the Scandinavian peoples that he even entertained the possibility of emigrating to Denmark or Sweden.

1933 A BOOKS - NONE

1933 B OTHER WRITINGS

1   PEARDON, THOMAS PRESTON. The Transition in English Historical Writing: 1760-1830. New York: Columbia University Press, pp. 177-181; 234-44.
    Peardon finds the spirit of nationalism in both Southey's Life of Nelson and the History of the Peninsular War in its anti-French sentiments and its glorification of English actions. In the History of Brazil Peardon praises the final chapter on the state of Brazil in 1809, the picture of the Jesuit society in Paraguay, and the realistic view of the life of the savages and the early settlers. Southey's Life of Wesley can be considered as history because of Southey's awareness of the historical importance of the Methodist movement which he delineated. In fact, the biography of Wesley and the Brazilian history "are Southey's chief claims to the title of historian." But Southey failed as an historian for want of thorough research, a failure to use research collections, and from too great a facility in composition.

2   WRIGHT, H. G. "Three Aspects of Southey." RES, 9, 37-46.
    Sees in Southey's description of the village of Caermadoc (in Madoc) a reminiscence of Southey's old dream of pantisocracy; Madoc also contains recollections of Coleridge and of Southey's journeys in Spain and Portugal.

1934 A BOOKS

1   EHRICH, EMIL. Southey und Landor: Eine Studie über ihre literarischen, geistigen und menschlichen Beziehungen. Göttingen, 212 pp.
    Covers every aspect of the Southey-Landor relationship with lengthy quotations from all sources. The study begins with Southey's review of Landor's Gebir (1798), describes their meeting in 1808, Landor's encouragement of Southey,

Southey's criticism of Count Julian, the connection between that poem and Roderick, Southey's share in the Imaginary Conversations, the similarities and dissimilarities of their views on literature, religion, politics, and their literary contemporaries. Ehrich has thoroughly searched the periodicals for contemporary criticisms (which he quotes) and has also cited passages of literary and social critics of the later nineteenth and twentieth centuries. The author had access to the manuscript letters of Southey to Landor in the Victoria and Albert Museum, for which he gives a calendar and of which he makes appropriate use in the study.

1934 B OTHER WRITINGS

1   GIBBS, W. E. "Unpublished Letters Concerning Cottle's Coleridge." PMLA, 49, 208-28.
    Describes the efforts of Coleridge's friends to prevent Cottle from publishing his Recollections. J. T. Coleridge sought Southey's aid in attempting to persuade Cottle to delete passages about Coleridge's use of opium. Southey's position was embarrassing and what happened is not clear, but see New Letters, II, 444-45 and notes (1965.A1).

2   LEWIS, N. B. "The Abolitionist Movement in Sheffield." BJRL, 18, 377-92.
    Southey's letter to Mrs. W. B. Rawson of May 4, 1833 shows that he believed in a slower method of abolition than that proposed by the emancipators.

3   "Olybrius." "Verses on Leigh Hunt by Southey and Dickens." N & Q, 166, 79.
    Quotes eleven lines in Southey's handwriting on verso of Hunt's "Abou ben Adhem."

4   POTTER, STEPHEN, ed. Minnow Among Tritons. London: Nonesuch Press.
    These letters of Mrs. S. T. Coleridge to Thomas Poole contain many references to Southey and life at Greta Hall.

1935 A BOOKS - NONE

1935 B OTHER WRITINGS

1   WEBER, C. A. Bristols Bedeutung für die Englische Romantik. Halle. Studien zur englischen Philologie. No. 89, 304 pp.
    Contains detailed information about the minor Bristolians whom Southey knew in his early years - these men are con-

1935

nected with the dissenters and share an interest in the new poetry and Gothic supernaturalism. Weber sees Dr. Thomas Beddoes as the central figure of this Bristol group.

1937 A BOOKS - NONE

1937 B OTHER WRITINGS

1   FLETCHER, IFAN KYRLE. "Robert Southey and Miss Seton." TLS, November 20 and December 4, pp. 896, 928.
    Excerpts from Southey's unpublished letters to Barbara Seton, an English lady, whom the Southeys met in Portugal.

1938 A BOOKS - NONE

1938 B OTHER WRITINGS

1   BROWN, W. C. "Robert Southey and the English Interest in the Near East." ELH, 5, 218-24.
    Shows that Southey was unsympathetic to Mohammedanism and the Near East and that parts of Thalaba are versified passages from the prose works cited in the notes to the poem.

2   CURRY, KENNETH. "Uncollected Translations of Michaelangelo by Wordsworth and Southey." RES, 14, 193-99.
    Supplies text of Wordsworth's and Southey's translations for Richard Duppa's Life of Michaelangelo (1807): a poem of nine stanzas in collaboration between Wordsworth and Southey and four short poems - three sonnets - by Southey.

3   MORLEY, EDITH J., ed. Henry Crabb Robinson on Books and Their Writers. London: Dent. Three volumes.
    The diaries of Robinson contain detailed accounts of his many meetings with Southey and his comments on Southey's writings. The thorough index to this work lists over a hundred references to Southey himself, his opinions, and Robinson's views of Southey's works.

1939 A BOOKS - NONE

1939 B OTHER WRITINGS

1   CHAMBERS, R. W. "Ruskin (And Others) On Byron." Man's Unconquerable Mind. London: Cape, pp. 311-41.
    Reprint of 1925.B1.

2   CURRY, KENNETH. "A Note on Colerige's Copy of Malthus."
    PMLA, 54, 613-15.
       Shows that Southey used and marked this copy (in the British Library); supplements G. R. Potter's article, "Unpublished Marginalia in Coleridge's Copy of Malthus's Essay on Population," PMLA, 51, 1061-68.

3   _____. "Southey's Contributions to the Annual Review." BB, 16, 195-97.
       A list of Southey's reviews in the Annual Review, 1802-08, derived from Southey's scrap book of these reviews in the British Library and the evidence in his correspondence.

4   SEARY, E. R. "Robert Southey and Ebenezer Elliott: Some New Southey Letters." RES, 15, 410-21.
       Four letters to Elliot, the Corn Law poet.

1940 A BOOKS - NONE

1940 B OTHER WRITINGS

1   BRIGHTFIELD, M. F. John Wilson Croker. Berkeley: University of California Press; London: Allen and Unwin, pp. 207-16.
       Croker and Southey first met in 1811. Croker frequently helped Southey: first, in an unsuccessful bid (1812) for the post of historiographer royal; secondly, in 1813 in securing the laureateship for him. Croker also gave Southey materials for the Nelson biography, and Southey on occasion consulted Croker about his laureate odes. Brightfield publishes for the first time several letters of Southey to Croker.

2   RENWICK, W. L. "Southeyana." DUJ, 2, 67-69.
       Renwick owned the manuscripts of Southey's letters to W. L. Bowles (mostly published in Greever's A Wiltshire Parson and His Friends, 1926.B2); prints several of these letters including a few excerpts not in Greever.

1941 A BOOKS - NONE

1941 B OTHER WRITINGS

1   CLINE, C. L. "The Correspondence of Robert Southey and Isaac D'Israeli." RES, 17, 65-79.
       Eleven letters (1822-37) discuss books, literary projects, but perhaps of most interest the exhumation of the remains of John Hampden.

1941

2 HOADLEY, FRANK T. "The Controversy Over Southey's Wat Tyler."
SP, 38, 81-96.
A full account of all the circumstances leading to the
piratical publication of this work in 1817 and the various
editions of the poem.

1942 A BOOKS - NONE

1942 B OTHER WRITINGS

1 BROUGHTON, L. N., ed. Some Letters of the Wordsworth Family,
Now First Published, with a Few Unpublished Letters of Coleridge and Southey and Others. Cornell Studies in English,
32. Ithaca: Cornell University Press, pp. 114-22.
Five letters by Southey with very full annotation.

2 CAMERON, K. N. "Shelley vs. Southey: New Light on an Old
Quarrel." PMLA, 57, 489-512.
Argues that Shelley had Southey in mind as the reviewer
attacked in Adonais and that Southey had attacked Shelley
(although not by name) in the Quarterly article, "Popular
Disaffection." Cameron rejects Southey's outright state-
ment that he had never referred to Shelley directly or in-
directly in his writings.

3 JARRETT-KERR, M. "Southey's Colloquies." Nineteenth Century,
132, 181-87.
Examines the Colloquies partly to offset Macaulay's criticism and to challenge the Whig view of history and concludes that Southey's vision of progress is more to present-
day taste than Macaulay's. The arrangement of the Colloquies is "sufficiently successful to convey a sense of tradition scrutinising novelty, and faith standing in judgment
upon unbelief, a sense of dignity which lacks the wit but
lacks also the superficiality of Macaulay."

1943 A BOOKS - NONE

1943 B OTHER WRITINGS

1 ANON. "Southey: A Problem of Romanticism - Poet Who Lost His
Way." TLS, March 20, p. 142.
The failure of Southey's poems is due to the fact that he
"lost his way to romance by treating his dreams as no part
of it."

1943

2   CURRY, KENNETH. "Southey's Madoc: The Manuscript of 1794."
    PQ, 22, 347-69.
        The text of the first two and a half books of the first
    draft - published here for the first time - is full of the
    same revolutionary, democratic sentiment and Miltonic blank
    verse as Joan of Arc. When the poem was published in 1805
    these elements had been eliminated through extensive revi-
    sion and rewriting.

3   DAVIS, SAMUEL. "A Centenary Appreciation of Southey's Life of
    Wesley." London Quarterly and Holborn Review, 168, 319-23.
        Davis praises Southey's treatment of Wesley as a human
    being rather than as a saint, but finds in Southey's own
    fundamental lack of sympathy for religious enthusiasm the
    basic flaw in what still remains the standard biography of
    Wesley.

4   ELWIN, MALCOLM. Letter to editor. TLS, March 27, p. 151.
        Response to 1943.B1. Points out influence of Southey
    upon Shelley and the importance of the reforms sponsored
    by Southey.

5   _____. "Robert Southey." Quarterly Review, 281, 187-201.
        A retelling of the story of Southey's life with some ac-
    count of his various books and his Quarterly articles.
    Elwin defends Southey from the attacks of Hazlitt, Byron,
    and especially Macaulay, but concludes: "In poetry, as in
    prose, Southey was too prolific to be popular."

6   HOWE, H. W. Greta Hall. Privately printed.
        A pamphlet giving a full and valuable account of Greta
    Hall, the home of the Southeys for forty years.

7   JEFFERY, SIDNEY. "Southey and Gilbert." TLS, March 20, p.
    139.
        A letter to William Roscoe, July 26, 1798.

8   SHAND, JOHN. "Robert Southey." Nineteenth Century, 133,
    138-41.
        Surveys Southey's career and concludes that his best work
    is his correspondence.

9   SOUSA-LEÃO, J. de. "Robert Southey." Revista do Instituto
    Histórico e Geografico Brasileiro, 178, 33-60.
        A full discussion of Southey's interest in Brazil, the
    complete text of the letters to the Koster family (with
    Portuguese translations), the portion of the catalogue of
    Southey's library devoted to Spanish and Portuguese items.
    Illustrated with several portraits of Southey and Greta Hall.

1943

10 _____. "Southey and Brazil." MLR, 38, 181-91.
A discussion of Southey's interest in Brazil and Portugal, his collection of manuscripts and books pertaining to those countries, and an account of his correspondence with John and Henry Koster.

1944 A BOOKS

1 EDMONDS, HARRY MORETON SOUTHEY. Homage to Southey. London: Sylvan Press.
Reprints seven short poems of Southey; eight original poems of Edmonds. The publisher gives two reasons for the volume: "Major Edmonds's direct connection with the Southey family" and "secondly, that his own poems are the impressions of first-hand experience in a varied and colourful career." Introduction by Henry Newnham; title page by John Farleigh.

1944 B OTHER WRITINGS

1 BAUGHMAN, ROLAND. "Southey the Schoolboy." HLQ, 7, 247-80.
An essay on Southey's days at Wesminster School based upon nine unpublished letters to his schoolfellow Charles Collins, 1791-93 (See 1967.B2).

2 BRIGHTFIELD, M. F. "Lockhart's Quarterly Contributors." PMLA, 59, 491-512.
Identifies from Murray's records the reviews written by Southey as well as the reviewers of Southey's books noticed in the Quarterly for the years 1826 to 1853. A listing without comment.

3 CURRY, KENNETH. "Southey's Visit to Caroline Wordsworth Baudouin." PMLA, 59, 599-602.
An account of Southey's visit to Wordsworth's French daughter (and granddaughter) in Paris during May, 1817. Reprinted in New Letters, II, 159-63 (1965.A1).

4 [ZANDVOORT, R. W.] "Two Unpublished Letters by Robert Southey." ES, 26, 6-10.
To the Reverend J. H. Halbertsma.

1945 A BOOKS

1 SIMMONS, JACK. Southey. London: Collins; New Haven: Yale University Press.

The emphasis of this study is biographical - the only full-length biography since Dowden's - and draws together material from widely scattered published sources and unpublished manuscripts. The arrangement is chronological, and Southey's relations with his famous contemporaries are emphasized as well as the impact of his writings upon the public. Simmons prefers Southey's prose to his poetry but praises Kehama, the ballads, and the short lyrics dealing with domestic life. Southey's unadorned prose style is commended with illustrative quotations from the Life of Nelson and the Colloquies. The book contains reproductions of several portraits (not hitherto reproduced), a list of Southey's published books, and a genealogical table. Informative footnotes direct the reader to many references not elsewhere available.

1945 B OTHER WRITINGS

1   ANON. "The Industrious Poet: In Southey's Workshop." TLS, April 21, p. 186.
    A review-article of Simmons' biography. The author finds (in Southey) "something intrinsically unlikeable in the work and in its author....His goodness, like the bulk of his poetry, lacks charm."

2   GRIGGS, E. L. "Robert Southey's Estimate of Samuel Taylor Coleridge: A Study in Human Relations." HLQ, 9, 61-94.
    Griggs, basing his article on the Rickman-Southey correspondence, finds Southey intolerant and jealous; obstructing moves of others seeking to help Coleridge; and remaining silent when he could have helped; and, finally, refusing to help the Coleridge family in writing about Coleridge after his death.

3   HAVENS, R. D. "Southey's Specimens of the Later English Poets." PMLA, 60, 1066-79.
    Points out the carelessness with which the book was printed and the inadequacies of the biographical-critical materials. The article is based upon the manuscript copy from which the printer worked. Those who seek to awaken interest in Southey "might well call attention to the epigrams, the incisive comments, the humor, and the curious anecdotes" found in the Specimens, of which Havens quotes several examples.

4   KERN, J. D., E. SCHNEIDER, and I. GRIGGS. "Lockhart to Croker on the Quarterly." PMLA, 60, 175-98.
    Contains notes and comments on three of Southey's Quarterly articles.

1946

1946 A BOOKS - NONE

1946 B OTHER WRITINGS

1. HAVENS, R. D. "Southey's Revision of his Life of Wesley." RES, 22, 134-36.
   Southey incorporated most of his extra notes on Wesley into this revision. The manuscript of this edition was in Havens' possession.

2. MACAULAY, ROSE. "A Romantic Among the Philistines." They Went to Portugal. London: Cape.
   Recounts Southey's visit to Portugal, objects to Southey's disapproval of so many Portuguese ways, and points out that Southey did not associate with the upper-class society of the British embassy.
   Reprinted from Orion, A Miscellany, I (1945), 6-16.

3. SCHILLING, B. N. "Southey." Human Dignity and the Great Victorians. New York: Columbia University Press, pp. 61-73.
   Although Southey has less power of thought than Coleridge he was "no less sincere, and we welcome his greater clarity." Southey was the "first of the literary humanitarians to complain of the industrial era on aesthetic grounds." He anticipated Kingsley in his emphasis upon the need for sanitary reform. Southey was deeply moved by the human cost - "the loss of kindly and generous feeling, of honor and integrity, the decay of the highest powers of man." Southey was unable to follow the socialist Robert Owen in his experiments because they were not founded upon a religious belief.

4. SHAMBURGER, M. I. and V. R. LACHMANN. "Southey and 'The Three Bears.'" JAF, 59, 400-403.
   Suggests that Southey's sources are "Sneewittchen" from Grimm's collection and a Norwegian tale from oral tradition of a king's daughter who finds a bear's cave, eats porridge from the table, and sleeps underneath a bed.

5. STARR, N. C. "Coleridge's 'Sir Leoline.'" PMLA, 61, 157-62.
   Persuasive argument for Southey as the friend in Coleridge's Christabel - "they had been friends in youth."

6. WILSON, J. L. "Washington Irving's 'Celebrated English Poet.'" AL, 18, 247-49.
   Suggests that Southey is the poet mentioned in the sketch of Philip of Pokanoket.

Robert Southey: A Reference Guide

1947 A BOOKS - NONE

1947 B OTHER WRITINGS

1   EARLY, BENJAMIN N. "A Volume by Robert Southey." CLQ, 2nd ser., August, pp. 37-39.
    An edition of Joan of Arc, Ballads, Lyrics and Minor Poems, published in 1873 by Lee and Shepard of Boston, an exact duplicate of an unauthorized English edition of Southey's poems published in "Routledge's British Poets" in 1853. Includes poems reprinted from the Annual Anthology that are not Southey's.

2   ELWIN, MALCOLM. The First Romantics. London: Macdonald; New York: Longmans Green.
    A biographical account of the lives of Wordsworth, Coleridge, and Southey to about 1803. Elwin is partial to Coleridge and sees Southey as responsible for Coleridge's disastrous marriage. Southey's own "infatuation for Edith had been for two years the one objective from which his faith had never shifted." This objective influenced his views of pantisocracy, his relations with Coleridge, and, of course, the secret marriage in 1795. The biography readily moves in an entertaining fashion from one writer to another and quotes freely from the published correspondence and memoirs concerning all three men.

1948 A BOOKS - NONE

1948 B OTHER WRITINGS

1   CURRY, KENNETH. "The Contributors to the Annual Anthology." PBSA, 42, 50-65.
    Identification of the authors who contributed (often anonymously) to this anthology edited by Southey (1799-1800); some information was derived from several copies which Southey had marked.

1949 A BOOKS - NONE

1949 B OTHER WRITINGS

1   BERNBAUM, ERNEST. Guide Through the Romantic Movement. Second Edition. New York: Ronald Press, pp. 154-64.
    Chapter on Southey outlines his career, lists the main qualities of his works, and evaluates them. Bernbaum finds

1949

one reason for Southey's secondary rank today in that "he overlooked a principle which Scott never left out of account - namely, that those aspects of past history are most important to us which have left a permanent impress upon our Anglo-American civilization." Bernbaum also includes a bibliography and topics for discussion and further study.

2   KEYNES, GEOFFREY. Blake Studies. London: Hart-Davis, pp. 90-93.
    Discusses all aspects of the Blake-Southey relationship. Southey met Blake through H. C. Robinson in 1811. Southey visited Blake, who showed him his unfinished Jerusalem. Southey remembered Blake later and quoted his "Mad Song" and "The Flea" in The Doctor.

3   SHINE, HILL and HELEN. The Quarterly Review Under Gifford: Identification of Contributors 1809-1824. Chapel Hill: University of North Carolina Press.
    Identification of articles by (and attributed to) Southey during 1809-24, the years of Gifford's editorship.

4   WHALLEY, GEORGE. "The Bristol Library Borrowings of Southey and Coleridge 1793-98." Library, 5th ser., 4, 114-32.
    This listing of the books borrowed by Southey and Coleridge supersedes and supplements Kaufman's list (1924.B1).

1950 A BOOKS - NONE

1950 B OTHER WRITINGS

1   CHOLMONDELEY, R. H., ed. The Heber Letters: 1783-1832. London: Batchworth Press, 335 pp., passim.
    Seven letters to Richard Heber, the great book collector, reveal their mutual interest in old books and Heber's willingness to assist Southey.

2   EHRENPREIS, IRVIN. "Southey to Coleridge, 1799." N & Q, 195, 124-26.
    Southey's letter of October 11, 1799; reprinted in New Letters, I, 200-203 (1965.A1).

3   WHALLEY, GEORGE. "Coleridge and Southey in Bristol, 1795." RES, n.s. I, 324-40.
    The crises over pantisocracy and Sara Fricker (whom Coleridge married) reveal the basic incompatibility of Southey and Coleridge, shown in Southey's "impatience of philosophy which became the keystone of the dyspathy which was soon

to separate the two poets." Both were also concerned with the problem of the poet - "the symbolic transmutation of experience," but Southey was unable to follow Coleridge, who later turned to Wordsworth. Southey stimulated Coleridge's interest in the poetic possibilities of travel literature and "twilight materials of nascent science."

4   WOODRING, CARL R. "Letters from Bernard Barton to Robert Southey." HLB, 4, 351-58.
    Letters to Southey from 1815 to 1838, often on subjects of Quaker interest.

1951 A BOOKS

1   SIMMONS, JACK, ed. Letters from England. London: Cresset Press.
    Only modern reprint. Full introduction and helpful notes.

1951 B OTHER WRITINGS

1   DOWDEN, W. S. "The Source of the Metempsychosis Motif in Southey's Thalaba." MLN, 66, 555-56.
    The source is from George Sale's Preliminary Discourse to his translation of the Qurán.

2   ANON. "The Three Bears." TLS, November 23, 1951, p. xiii (Children's Section).
    Describes a rhymed version of the story by Eleanor Mure preserved in a manuscript dated September 26, 1831. Suggests that the tale was a folk tale known to both the Mure and Southey families.

1952 A BOOKS - NONE

1952 B OTHER WRITINGS

1   CARNALL, GEOFFREY. "A Note on Southey's Later Religious Opinions." PQ, 31, 399-406.
    Southey, although not always doctrinally at home in the Church, was interested in the social value of religions, and supported the Established Church as a bulwark against fanaticism and as a source of social stability. Southey did not believe in the damnation of the wicked in eternal torment and accepted the possibility of salvation outside the Christian fold. Southey also supported Christian missions for their social value. As he grew older he tended towards greater orthodoxy.

1953

1953 A BOOKS

1   HARVEY, E. R. H., ed. <u>The Life of Nelson</u>. Macdonald Illustrated Classics. London: Macdonald.
    Contains introduction, notes, and an appendix on the Naples Controversy.

1953 B OTHER WRITINGS

1   CURRY, KENNETH. "Two New Works of Southey." <u>SB</u>, 5, 197-200.
    The two works are: <u>An Exposure of the Misrepresentations and Calumnies in Mr. Marsh's Review of Sir George Barlow's Administration at Madras</u> (1813) and an annotated edition (1809) of J. I. Molina's <u>The Geographical, Natural, and Civil History of Chili...to which are added, Notes from the Spanish and French Version, and Two Appendixes by the English editor</u>. Published by Longman in two volumes.

2   ZALL, P. M. "Lord Eldon's Censorship." <u>PMLA</u>, 68, 436-43.
    Eldon's refusal of Southey's claim against Sherwood, the piratical publisher of <u>Wat Tyler</u>, on the ground that a "person cannot recover in damages for a work which is, in its nature, calculated to do injury to the public" had important consequences for similar cases involving Shelley and Byron. The judgment reflects Eldon's own peculiar point of view and anticipates what is often thought of as a typically "Victorian" attitude.

1954 A BOOKS - NONE

1954 B OTHER WRITINGS

1   CLINE, C. L. "Byron and Southey: A Suppressed Rejoinder." <u>KSJ</u>, 3, 27-38.
    Byron wrote a letter (never sent) to the <u>Courier</u> on February 5, 1822 in reply to Southey's letter in the <u>Courier</u> (January 6, 1821). Byron's letter is published here for the first time.

2   HOPKINS, KENNETH. "Robert Southey." <u>The Poets Laureate</u>. London: Bodley Head, pp. 124-44.
    Combines a biographical account of Southey with a discussion of his work as laureate. Southey thought that the laureate should write an ode when the occasion demanded one rather than doing the required official odes: these were, however, written, the music composed, but they were usually neither performed nor published.

1955

3   KADERLY, N. L. "Southey's Borrowings from Celia Fiennes." MLN, 69, 249-53.
    The travel journals of Celia Fiennes have been edited by Christopher Morris (Cresset Library, 1949). The manuscript, once owned by Southey, was used by him in Omniana (in passages reprinted from his articles in the Athenaeum), and it also proved helpful in writing the Espriella Letters.

4   SERONSY, C. C. "Marginalia by Coleridge in Three Copies of His Published Works." SP, 51, 470-81.
    Coleridge marked a copy of his Conciones ad Populum (1795), now in the Harvard Library, stating that the poem "To the Exiled Patriots" was by Southey. See also Marcus (1932.B3) who discusses this poem and its background.

5   SUPER, R. H. Walter Savage Landor. New York: New York University Press.
    This chronologically arranged biography records all the meetings between Landor and Southey as they occurred together with quotations from their correspondence. Super also describes Landor's efforts in behalf of Southey's family after his death and his work in memorializing Southey.

1955 A BOOKS - NONE

1955 B OTHER WRITINGS

1   CARNALL, GEOFFREY. "Southey and Quakerism." Friends' Quarterly, 9, 31-40.
    Southey, who was acquainted with such Quakers as Bernard Barton and Joseph John Gurney, had described himself in 1807 as "very nearly a Quaker." Southey planned to write a biography of George Fox, and in his unfinished poem, Oliver Newman, he had a Quaker hero. Although Southey supported the Church of England, he did not assent to all its doctrines. Southey failed to explore the contradictions in his religious beliefs - at one time he had been drawn to Quakerism because it seemed to open up the way to his criticism of the Established Church. But Southey lost interest in theological issues and did not explore them. Carnall quotes briefly from the manuscripts of Southey's unfinished life of Fox and Gurney's diary - in Friends' House, London.

2   KADERLY, N. L. "Southey and the Quarterly Review." MLN, 70, 261-63.
    John Rickman wrote the article, "Poor Laws" in the Quarterly for January, 1818; Southey, the article, "On the

1955

        Means of Improving the People" in the issue for April, 1818. Clarifies the entries by Shine (1949.B3) for these articles. Southey's letter to Rickman (New Letters, II, 178, 1965.A1) also makes the issue clear.

3   McELDERRY, B. R., JR. "Southey and Wordsworth's 'The Idiot Boy.'" N & Q, 200, 490-91.
        Southey's "Idiot" in the Morning Post (not reprinted by Southey, but certainly by him) presents a contrast to Wordsworth's poem. Southey's poem is printed here. Carnall (1956.B1) agrees with the conclusion and the interpretation.

1956 A BOOKS - NONE

1956 B OTHER WRITINGS

1   CARNALL, GEOFFREY. "'The Idiot Boy.'" N & Q, 201, 81-82.
        Continues McElderry's article (N & Q, 1955.B3). Accepts the attribution of the poem to Southey, but points out that Southey's idiot boy "was a deserving object of pity; Wordsworth's boy was not."

2   KING, R. W. "A Note on Shelley, Gibbon, Voltaire and Southey." MLR, 51, 225-27.
        Suggests that Shelley's sentence "I mean that record of crimes and miseries, History" came not directly from Gibbon or Voltaire but from Southey's poem "History" and its phrase "Thou chronicle of crimes!/I'll read no more."

3   METZDORF, R. F. "Southey Manuscripts at Yale." YULG, 30, 157-62.
        An account of an important collection of Southey manuscripts, including Roderick, Madoc, The Curse of Kehama, and Amadis of Gaul.

4   SELIG, K. L. "Sabuco de Nantes, Feijóo and Robert Southey." MLN, 71, 415-16.
        Quotes the autograph note by Southey in his copy of Dona Oliva Sabuco de Nantes' Nueva filosofia de la naturaleza del hombre (1557). Southey devotes several chapters to Dona Oliva in The Doctor.

5   SCHRICKX, W. "Een Onuitgegeven Brief van Robert Southey." RLV, 22, 144-46.
        A letter to the librarian of the Gent public library, October 24, 1815.

1957 A BOOKS - NONE

1957 B OTHER WRITINGS

1   CURRY, KENNETH. "Southey." English Romantic Poets and Essayists: A Review of Research. Edited by C. W. and L. H. Houtchens. New York: Modern Language Association, pp. 158-87.
    A narrative survey of research and criticism arranged under the subheads of bibliographies, editions, biographies, criticism, and Spain and Portugal. This essay evaluates the books and essays under review and groups together the items on similar topics. The series to which this book belongs is designed for the graduate student and to offer him guidance and suggestions among the multiplicity of books and articles. The discussion in this chapter may be used as a supplement to the entries in this present volume in the Reference Guide Series. A revised edition of this chapter (and book) appeared in 1966 (See 1966.B1).

1958 A BOOKS

1   Chronicle of the Cid. Introduction by V. S. Pritchett. Illustrations by René Ben Sussan. New York: Heritage Press.
    A beautifully printed and illustrated edition. Introduction surveys Southey's career and discusses the background of the Cid.

1958 B OTHER WRITINGS

1   ALLCHIN, A. M. The Silent Rebellion: Anglican Religious Communities 1845-1900. London: S C M Press, pp. 39-43.
    When Southey's hope that religious houses in England for women would be established under the auspices of the Church of England was realized in 1845, W. E. Gladstone included a quotation from the Colloquies in the prospectus for such a house. Lord John Manners had recommended in 1843 the establishment of a Sisterhood of Mercy as a memorial to Southey. His Colloquies continued throughout the century to be a source of reference and quotation for those interested in the establishment of religious communities in the Anglican Church not only for women, but also for men.

2   OBER, WARREN U. "'Mohammed': The Outline of a Proposed Poem by Coleridge and Southey." N & Q, 203, 448.
    Outline of poem has connections with "Kubla Khan" (See 1959.B2).

1958

3 WILLIAMS, RAYMOND. "Robert Southey and Robert Owen." Culture and Society. London: Allen and Unwin; New York: Columbia University Press, pp. 20-29.
   A comparison of Southey's Colloquies and Owen's Observations reveals many points of similarity. Both were paternalistic in their suggested remedies, and if Owen led to socialism and cooperatives, Southey led to the new conservatism and the Young England movement for which Southey's Colloquies served as a text.

1959 A BOOKS

1 CABRAL, ADOLFO. Southey e Portugal: 1774-1801. Lisbon. P. Fernandes.
   A full account of Southey's residence and travels in Portugal together with a description of his books and articles dealing with Portuguese history and literature. Written in Portuguese.

1959 B OTHER WRITINGS

1 METZDORF, R. F., ed. The Tinker Library. New Haven: Yale University Library.
   Lists and describes many manuscripts, autograph letters, and first editions of Southey - now in the Yale Library.

2 OBER, WARREN U. "Southey, Coleridge and 'Kubla Khan.'" JEGP, 58, 414-22.
   Detailed evidence showing that Southey through his poetry and reading gave Coleridge much material for 'Kubla Khan' (See 1958.B2).

1960 A BOOKS

1 CABRAL, ADOLFO, ed. Robert Southey: Journals of a Residence in Portugal 1800-1801 and a Visit to France in 1838. Oxford: Clarendon Press.
   These journals expand considerably our knowledge of Southey's travels. The Portuguese journal describes his two long trips: the first northwards to Coimbra from Lisbon and the second southwards to Tavira and Faro near the Spanish border. The journals describe religious processions and ceremonies, fireworks, churches, castles, towns, mountains, and the persons encountered along the way. The French journal, written at the end of Southey's career, still shows his eye for interesting detail. The annotation of these

volumes is thorough, and, since the editor was himself Portuguese, especially interesting for the Portuguese section.

2 CARNALL, GEOFFREY. Robert Southey and His Age: The Development of a Conservative Mind. Oxford: Clarendon Press.
A wide-ranging survey of Southey's political ideas based upon an extensive exploration of his books and his reviews in the Annual Review, the Quarterly Review, and the first four volumes of the Edinburgh Annual Register (where Southey wrote the History of the Year for 1808-11). Not only does Carnall present the background of national and international politics but also the psychological atmosphere of the age which communicated to Southey feelings of anxiety, depression, loneliness, and misanthropy. Carnall explores many significant topics in considerable depth such as pantisocracy, missionaries, Methodists, small religious sects, Southey's own religious beliefs (difficult to pinpoint), the Malthusian controversy, Peterloo, Wat Tyler, Robert Owen, the Reform legislation, Catholic Emancipation, and the warfare between the Edinburgh Review and the Quarterly Review. A special feature of this study is the inclusion of fresh quotations from Southey's works - especially from his reviews. The book contains reproductions of two new portraits of Southey by Edward Nash.

1960 B OTHER WRITINGS

1 PARKER, W. M. "Southey's Politics and Travels." Quarterly Review, 298, 333-45.
A review-article of books by Cabral and Carnall with especial mention of Southey and the Quarterly.

2 SHAVER, CHESTER L. "Wordsworth on Byron: An Unpublished Letter to Southey." MLN, 75, 488-90.
Southey consulted Wordsworth about his reply to Byron's attack upon him in The Two Foscari: Wordsworth gives advice as to how attack Byron.

1961 A BOOKS

1 DeQUINCEY, THOMAS. Reminiscences of the English Lake Poets. Introduction and notes by John E. Jordan. Everyman's Library. London: Dent.
Reprints chapters about Southey from the text in Tait's.

1961

1961 B OTHER WRITINGS

1 CURRY, KENNETH. "The Library of Robert Southey." <u>Studies in Honor of J. C. Hodges and Alwin Thaler</u> (Special number of <u>Tennessee Studies in Literature</u>), pp. 77-86.
   A survey of the formation, scope, and dispersal of Southey's library of 14,000 books and Portuguese manuscripts.

2 PATTERSON, C. I. "The Keats-Hazlitt-Hunt Copy of <u>Palmerin of England</u> in Relation to Keats's Poetry." <u>JEGP</u>, 60, 31-43.
   Keats, who had marked twenty-four pages of text in this copy of Southey's edition of <u>Palmerin</u>, derived much material for his poems from this book. Parallels with passages from his poetry indicate the many possible influences.

3 SHUMAN, R. BAIRD. "Southey to Dyer: An Unpublished Letter." <u>N & Q</u>, 206, 14-15.
   Letter to George Dyer (March 27, 1800) is from a manuscript in the library of Pennington School, New Jersey.

1962 A BOOKS

1 <u>Life of Nelson</u>. Introduction by Carola Oman. Everyman Library. London: Dent; New York: E. P. Dutton.
   The brief introduction is complemented by an index.

1962 B OTHER WRITINGS - NONE

1963 A BOOKS - NONE

1963 B OTHER WRITINGS

1 BEYER, W. W. "Southey, Orientalism and <u>Thalaba</u>." <u>The Enchanted Forest</u>. Oxford: Blackwell, pp. 234-45.
   Detailed parallels between <u>Thalaba</u> and Wieland's <u>Oberon</u>. William Taylor had introduced Southey to <u>Oberon</u>.

2 GORDAN, J. D. "New in the Berg Collection: 1959-61." <u>BNYPL</u>, 67, 626-27.
   A brief account of some Southey manuscripts in the collection: the letters to Lord Shaftesbury, William Wilberforce, William Westall, and several single letters.

1964 A BOOKS - NONE

1964 B OTHER WRITINGS

1 BRAEKMAN, W. "Letters by Robert Southey to Sir John Taylor Coleridge." SGG, 6, 103-230.
    Forty-four letters to Coleridge with an index of names.

2 CARNALL, GEOFFREY. Robert Southey. British Council's Writers and Their Works Series. No. 176. London: Longmans.
    A brief introduction to Southey's life and career. Contains a bibliography and a reproduction of Lawrence's portrait of Southey.

3 VAN DONGEN, C. "Robert Southey's Reis door Holland in 1825." LT, No. 225, pp. 371-79.
    Describes Southey's visit to the Netherlands where he was a guest in the home of Willem Bilderdijk. This article quotes not only Southey's letters describing his visit but also Bilderdijk's account and an extract from Willem de Clerq's diary, who remarked that Southey appeared as an industrious, tireless writer rather than a man of genius.

1965 A BOOKS

1 CURRY, KENNETH, ed. New Letters of Robert Southey. New York: Columbia University Press. Two volumes.
    Prints about five hundred new letters including a few (notably some to Cottle) previously available only in garbled form; biographical sketches of Southey's friends and principal correspondents comprise twenty-eight pages; the annotation has additional details about additions to the canon of Southey's writings. These letters expand our knowledge of Southey's life, career, the progress of his ideas, and the genesis and composition of his books and articles.

1965 B OTHER WRITINGS

1 NOWELL-SMITH, SIMON. "Query 186. Southey, Lamb and Joan of Arc." BC, 14, 82.
    Describes a large paper copy of the second edition of Joan of Arc (1798), a presentation copy from Southey to Lamb.

2 OBER, KENNETH H. and WARREN U. OBER. "Žukovskij's Early Translation of the Ballads of Robert Southey." SEEJ, 9, 181-90.

1965

> Žukovskij translated into Russian many English poems including Gray's "Elegy" and poems by Byron, Moore, and Scott. His translations of Southey include "Donica," "Mary, the Maid of the Inn," "Rudiger," "Queen Orraca," and "The Old Woman of Berkeley." The philosophy of translation of Žukovskij was: "A translator in prose is a slave, a translator in verse is a rival." The Obers maintain that Žukovskij's translations of Southey's ballads improve the originals. Russian translations of Southey's poems are provided.

1966 A BOOKS - NONE

1966 B OTHER WRITINGS

1 CURRY, KENNETH. "Robert Southey." The English Romantic Poets and Essayists: A Review of Research and Criticism. Ed. C. W. and L. H. Houtchens. Revised Edition. New York: New York University Press, pp. 155-82.
   A revised and up-dated version of the 1957 chapter.

2 FAHEY, DAVID M. "Southey's Review of Hallam." N & Q, 211, 178-79.
   Pp. 250 to 259 of the review are by the Reverend Mr. Edwards who "provided a commentary on some of the subjects Southey had omitted - Cromwell, the Restoration Whigs, and William III."

3 KROEBER, KARL. "Trends in Minor Romantic Narrative Poetry." Some British Romantics. Columbus: Ohio State University Press, pp. 269-92.
   Southey's epic-like narratives are connected with the spirit of Ossian, Percy, and Chatterton. Southey never achieved a narrative "that blends 'wonder' and 'history' into a poetic substance that is neither purely fabulous nor purely historical." Kroeber finds Southey's poetry "tedious." He also finds him incapable of lyric passion or dramatic excitement. "He has few ideas, his sensibility is often coarse, and his moral imagination is frequently conventional. But he conducts a narrative competently, and, in his early works (especially Joan of Arc and Kehama) he embellishes his stories with happily flamboyant imagery."

4 MARTIN, RICHARD T. "Robert Southey's Copy of Simon Browne's A Defence of the Religion of Nature." BNYPL, 70, 325-26.
   Southey used this work in chapter ten of his edition of Cowper. The book is in the Ohio State University Library.

5   REED, JOSEPH W., JR. "Southey's Nelson." English Biography in the Early Nineteenth Century 1801-1838. New Haven: Yale University Press, pp. 83-101.
    Southey's biography of Nelson "is an attempt to present the whole of a man who heeded a different drummer, who formed his life upon rules and conditions of a nonwordly ideal, but who still spoke the language of men, had a powerful hold upon men, experienced human frustration, bitterness, and the adversity of a world which neither recognized his ideal nor properly rewarded his achievements." Reed observes that Southey "succeeded, somehow, in satisfying Virginia Woolf's impossible criterion; he joined the granite of fact to the rainbow of personality."

1967 A BOOKS - NONE

1967 B OTHER WRITINGS

1   CURRY, KENNETH. "The Published Letters of Southey: A Checklist." BNYPL, 71, 158-64.
    Contains a listing of 124 books and articles containing letters by Southey together with an index of the names of the addressees.

2   MARPLES, MORRIS. "Southey at Westminster (1788-92)." Romantics at School: The Schooldays of Wordsworth, Coleridge, Southey, Byron, Shelley, and Keats. London: Faber; New York: Barnes and Noble, pp. 76-111.
    Not only a full account of Southey's schooling at Westminster but also at the Bristol schools he previously attended. Despite the value he derived from his attendance at Westminster - chiefly from the lifelong friendships established there - Southey was no friend to public schools and recommended either a day school or private tuition. Southey "condemns them repeatedly as nurseries of tyranny and brutality, inimical to religion and fatal to morality." See also Baughman (1944.B1) for further details of Southey's Westminster schooling.

3   MARTIN, C. G. "Southey: Two Unpublished Letters." N & Q, 212, 295.
    The two letters are to Tom Southey.

1968 A BOOKS

1   RAIMOND, JEAN. Robert Southey: L'homme et son temps. L'oeuvre. Le Role. (Etudes Anglaises 28). Paris: Didier, 667 pp.

1968

This lengthiest of studies solely devoted to Southey is divided into three parts: biography; a discussion of Southey's poetry and prose; and a concluding assessment. Raimond's goal has been to enhance the reputation of Southey, to call attention to his appealing aspects, and to explain his many failures. He recommends Southey's Life of Nelson, Life of Wesley, The Doctor (in FitzGerald's one-volume abridgement), Roderick, a few short poems, the three travel journals, and the letters. Raimond's method is to analyze each work according to a set pattern: summary, study of influence or source, and then judicial criticism. Although the length of this study may prove intimidating, these seven topics should be noted: (1) Southey as autobiographer; (2) the analysis of Roderick; (3) the explanation for the failures of the History of the Peninsular War and the Colloquies; (4) the analysis of the prose of the Life of Nelson; (5) the detailed verbal criticism of Southey's early poetry and its relationship to Wordsworth's poems; (6) the sketch of Southey's literary criticism; (7) the studies of Southey's vocabulary scattered throughout the study.

Raimond especially emphasizes Southey's skill as a biographer and as an autobiographer. In his discussion of Southey's autobiographical writings, Raimond includes not only the travel journals, the letters and the Espriella Letters, but much of the Colloquies and The Doctor, the latter of which he interprets as thinly disguised autobiography, for here the most clearly sketched character is the author himself. The letters are especially commended for their view of a changing society and for the chance to read a self-portrait of a man at all stages of his life. Raimond is harsher in his judgment of the poetry than of the prose, and attributes the failure of Joan of Arc to its ineffective use of images and similes. Roderick he commends for its suspenseful action with characters both human and culpable. The best parts of the histories are the biographical sketches. Little is said of Southey's contributions to periodicals including the Quarterly, and his work for the first four volumes of the Edinburgh Annual Register is ignored.

1968 B OTHER WRITINGS

1   OBER, WARREN U. "The Three Bears from Southey to Tolstoy." BNYPL, 72, 659-67.
    Surveys and comments upon the articles and remarks about the story and describes Tolstoy's translation into Russian (in his The New Alphabet, a collection of stories for children). In Tolstoy's version the bears are "a cozy little

family." Although he has omitted Southey's didacticism he has retained Southey's typographical tricks in the speeches of the bears.

2   POLLIN, B. R. "Southey's 'Battle of Blenheim' Parodied in the Morning Chronicle - a Whig Attack on the Battle of Copenhagen." BNYPL, 72, 507-17.
    Quotes "A Danish Tale (A la Southey)" from the Chronicle of March 26, 1808. Discussion of the political background and controversy over the battle of Copenhagen (See 1969.B2 and 1969.B5).

3   TILNEY, CHRYSTAL. "Robert Southey at Maes-Gwyn, 1802." NLWJ, 15, 437-50.
    Suggests that Southey's failure to secure a lease on the house at Maes-Gwyn was owing to the landlord's suspicion of Southey's republican views.

1969 A BOOKS

1   GITTINGS, ROBERT, Ed. Omniana; or, Horae Otiosiores. Fontwell: Centaur Press; Carbondale: Southern Illinois University Press.
    Contains introduction; only reprint of this 1812 collaboration between Southey and Coleridge.

1969 B OTHER WRITINGS

1   CARNALL, GEOFFREY. "Robert Southey" in The New Cambridge Bibliography of English Literature. Cambridge: Cambridge University Press, III, 254-61.
    The most complete listing of bibliographies, collections, letters, books, and articles on Southey.

2   _____. "Robert Southey and Thomas Moore on the Battle of Copenhagen." BNYPL, 73, 10-12.
    Suggests Thomas Moore as author of "A Danish Tale" (See 1968.B2; 1969.B5).

3   HAYDEN, JOHN O. The Romantic Reviewers: 1802-1824. Chicago: University of Chicago Press (Title page, 1968, but not published until 1969), pp. 111-23; 292-96.
    Surveys the critical reception of Southey's works, group by group, for this period. Southey's writings always received serious attention, and his contemporary critics, like later ones, esteemed his prose higher than his poetry. The subject matter of the long poems posed problems for the

1969

reviewers, both subject and diction being censured. Despite this criticism, neither the poet nor his work was rejected, and most reviewers gave testimony to his genius. Jeffrey in the Edinburgh Review was "much more tolerant when dealing with Southey than with Wordsworth, and consequently delivered much more intelligent and acceptable judgments." The favorable reviews stressed the occasional passage of beauty in the long poems and Southey's talent for descriptive verse. An appendix lists the reviews of Southey's works and indicates, when known, the name of the reviewer. Hayden, however, has very little on Southey himself as a reviewer of other writers. The book also contains a discussion of reviewing and of the principal reviews during the years 1802-24.

4   MERCHANT, PAUL. "Southey's 'St. Patrick's Purgatory' - An Unpublished Manuscript." Alta: The University of Birmingham Review, 2, 147-52.
    A facsimile of the manuscript together with a collation of the text as it appeared in Lewis' Tales of Wonder (1801) and the collected Poetical Works (1837).

5   POLLIN, B. R. "Lord Byron as Parodist of 'The Battle of Blenheim.'" BNYPL, 73, 215-17.
    Suggests that Byron was the author of the poem "A Danish Tale" in the Morning Chronicle (See 1968.B2; 1929.B2).

6   RAMAMURTY, K. "Robert Southey: The Development of His Poetic Art." Calcutta Review, 1, n.s., 305-20.
    Examples (with comments) on Southey's use of metaphors, images, and similes from both his long and short poems. His "figurative passages speak of Southey's firm hold on concrete fact."

1970 A BOOKS

1   COTTLE, JOSEPH. Reminiscences of Samuel Taylor Coleridge and Robert Southey. 1847. London: Lime Tree Bower. Facsimile reprint.

2   GRIGSON, GEOFFREY, ed. A Choice of Robert Southey's Verse. London: Faber, 112 pp.
    A small collection of Southey's short poems with a brief introduction. Southey "could be gay on the surface, charmingly inconsequent, and full of nonsense." Stresses Southey's happy year of 1798 at Westbury when he wrote many of his memorable short lyrics and ballads included in this selection.

1970 B OTHER WRITINGS

1   MARTIN, C. G. "Robert Southey: An Unpublished Letter."
    N & Q, 215, 378-79.
    To the historian William Coxe, April 25, 1818.

1971 A BOOKS

1   CAHN, HERBERT, ed. History of Brazil. New edition with preface and biography. New York: Lenox Hill Publishing Co. (Burt Franklin). Three volumes.
    Unseen. A review by William B. Lethbridge (TWC, VI, 199) points out serious errors in the biographical sketch of Southey.

1971 B OTHER WRITINGS

1   BROWN, SIMON. "Ebenezer Elliott and Robert Southey: Southey's Break with the Quarterly Review." RES, n.s. 22, 307-11.
    Lockhart omitted the part of Southey's review dealing with Elliott's poetry, publishing only that part on the Corn Laws. "The cutting of the Elliott article proved the climax of a growing discontent" with the Quarterly.

2   GEORGE, DAVID. "Two Manuscript Poems by Southey and Wordsworth." N & Q, 216, 376-77.
    An unpublished poem of thirteen lines dated October 1, 1821.

3   JACOBUS, MARY. "Southey's Debt to Lyrical Ballads (1798)." RES, n.s. 22, 20-36.
    A comparison of Southey's poems with those in Lyrical Ballads reveals the outstanding qualities of that work since Southey was using many of the same themes, devices, and stylistic mannerisms. Southey's poems in the Morning Post show that he made a popular and topical appeal from the same materials as those used in Lyrical Ballads.

4   MORGAN, PETER F. "Southey on Poetry." TLS, 16, 77-89.
    Surveys Southey's writings to find his views on poetry and modern English literary history. Southey stresses the importance of morality with feeling and purity of expression. He rejects the heroic couplet for blank verse and experimental forms. In his view of English poetical history he believes that the greatness found in Chaucer, Spenser, Shakespeare, and Milton received a severe blow during the Puritan revolution and the Restoration. Southey assigns

1971

Dryden and Pope a secondary rank and welcomed the improvement in poetry - also in public morality - seen in Cowper's and Wordsworth's poetry. But their achievement is "threatened by the immorality, excess of feeling, and technical elaboration in the poetry of Byron and his followers." Southey regards poetry "as a transparent medium for the expression of the elevated and moralized emotion of the poet." Morgan concludes that Southey deserves attention as a critic for his insights into poetic technique together with his high estimation of the poetic calling.

5 SANDERSON, DAVID R. "Robert Southey and the Standard Georgian Style." MQ, 12, 335-52.
   Finds Southey's prose style representative of the standard English style. A contrast with Goldsmith's shows that Southey's has a wider diction and deals more with concrete objects. His emphasis upon the qualities of things leads to a static quality - his use of the passive voice and various forms of the verb "to be" - these show him in contrast to Hazlitt and De Quincey who showed in their style more action and violent movement.

1972 A BOOKS

1 MADDEN, LIONEL, ed. Robert Southey: The Critical Heritage. Critical Heritage Series. London and Boston: Routledge and Kegan Paul.
   Reprints 144 reviews and comments on Southey's works and life from 1794 to 1879, including not only formally published reviews and studies but also passages from letters and memoirs. Poems, usually parodies, are also included. The first review is from the Critical Review (1794) and the last an excerpt from Dowden's biography (1879). A thirty-one page introduction surveys Southey's critical reputation according to such classification as epics, laureate poems and Wat Tyler, prose writings, reputation abroad, Southey's finances, posthumous reputation to 1879, and reputation after 1879 with frequent citation and quotation from the selections in the anthology.

2 SOUTHEY, ROBERT. The Origin, Nature and Object of the New System of Education. Clifton, N. J.: Augustus M. Kelley.
   A reprint of the rare pamphlet of 1812, which was an expansion of an article in the Quarterly (August, 1811).

1972 B OTHER WRITINGS

1   ELIAS, ROBERT H. and MICHAEL N. STANTON. "Thomas Atwood Digges and Adventures of Alonso: Evidence from Robert Southey." AL, 44, 118-22.
    The evidence of Digges's authorship is from the rough draft of the manuscript of Southey's autobiographical letters (University of Rochester). Digges was in Lisbon in 1774 and appears as a suitor of Southey's aunt, Miss Elizabeth Tyler.

2   LLORÉNS, VICENTE. "Blanco White and Robert Southey: Fragments of a Correspondence." SIR, 11, 147-52.
    Publishes Southey's first letter to White (November 4, 1811) and White's letter to Southey (June 15, 1822) which acknowledges White's indebtedness in his Doblado's Letters from Spain to Southey's Espriella Letters.

3   WARD, WILLIAM S. Literary Reviews in British Periodicals 1798-1820. New York: Garland Publishing Co. II, 512-17.
    Lists reviews of Southey's works in British periodicals for these years and contains entries not found in John O. Hayden's The Romantic Reviewers 1802-1824 (See 1969.B3).

1973 A BOOKS - NONE

1973 B OTHER WRITINGS

1   MONTLUZIN, EMILY LORRAINE DE. "Southey's 'Satanic School' Remarks: An Old Charge for a New Offender." KSJ, 21-22, 29-33.
    Many of Southey's remarks about Byron as leader of the Satanic School in the preface to his Vision of Judgement (1821) were not originally written with Byron in mind, but rather Thomas Moore. The remarks come, almost verbatim, from Southey's review of Moore's Epistles, Odes, and other Poems in the Annual Review (1806) condemning Moore's poems.

2   ROGERS, FRED. "Three Classic Nursery Tales." Redbook Magazine, 142 (December), 45-46.
    Reprints the original version of "The Story of the Three Bears" from The Doctor with illustrations. Points out the later changes in the story with the substitution of Goldilocks for the old woman. "It's the adult [in the person of the meddlesome old woman] who's the intrusive one in this version, not the naughty, childlike Goldilocks. In truth, Robert Southey must have known very well - probably intimately - the hidden feelings of children."

1974

1974 A BOOKS - NONE

1974 B OTHER WRITINGS

1 ANTIPPAS, ANDY P. "Four New Southey Letters." TWC, 5, 91-96.
Letters to Cottle, May, and Mrs. Clarkson with a facsimile of the Cottle letter.

2 BERNHARDT-KABISCH, ERNEST. "Southey in the Tropics: A Tale of Paraguay and the Problems of Romantic Faith." TWC, 5, 97-104.
A full account of Southey's last long poem, and one which shows Southey's failure as a poet: "he could confront the terror of reality so long as he could preserve the detachment of the mere chronicle." Furthermore, "myth-making thus becomes in his hands a means of merely evading human pain and paradox rather than of transmuting and transfiguring them."

3 CURRY, KENNETH. "Southey's Portraits." TWC, 5, 67-71.
The first listing of the many known portraits and drawings of Southey with an account of their history, the engravings made from the portraits, their present location, and sources of reproduction. Portraits known to have been made, but which are presently "lost" are also discussed.

4 GAINES, BARRY. "The Editions of Malory in the Early Nineteenth Century." PBSA, 68, 1-17.
Southey's two-volume edition of Malory's Morte D'Arthur, a reprint of Caxton's first edition, played an important role in the nineteenth-century revival of interest in Malory. Such writers as Burne-Jones, Morris, and Rossetti knew Malory through Southey's edition.

5 MORGAN, PETER F. "Southey: A Critical Spectrum." TWC, 5, 71-75.
A survey of Southey's writings for his views on poetry and English literary history. Southey stresses poetic morality, poetic feeling, and purity of expression and rejects - with Wordsworth and Coleridge - the Augustan heroic couplet in favor of blank verse and experimental forms. Southey views the Puritan revolution and the cavalier reaction as a blow to the poetic tradition of Chaucer, Spenser, Shakespeare, and Milton. Dryden and Pope are poets of the second rank, but an improvement came with Cowper and Wordsworth - an improvement "threatened by the immorality, excess of feeling, and technical elaboration in the poetry of Byron and his followers." In prose Southey's ideal was

"truth of subject matter and the plain style of presenting it." He was opposed to faultfinding reviewing for which he would substitute "an ideal of sympathy and fairness and his own generally genial practice."

6   OBER, WARREN U. and KENNETH H. "Žukovskij and Southey's Ballads: the Translator as Rival." TWC, 5, 76-88.
    This distinguished translator of English works into Russian translated eight of Southey's ballads, introducing some changes. "A personal and immediate involvement with his themes and characters and a real talent for choosing the vivid image and the right supplementary detail to bring some aspect of the original poem into sharper focus enable Žukovskij, at his best, to translate Southey's ballads into poems which have taken their place in his own country's literature."

7   PARK, ROY, ed. Sale Catalogues of Eminent Persons. Poets and Men of Letters. London: Mansell with Sotheby Parke Bernet Publications, pp. 75-288.
    Contains a reproduction of the British Library's copy of the Sale Catalogue of Southey's library sold during May, 1844 at Sotheby's. Park has written an introduction on Southey and his books, and E. M. Wilson has written a "Note" on the Spanish-Portuguese portion of the library.

8   PROUDFIT, CHARLES L. "Southey and Landor: A Literary Friendship." TWC, 5, 105-12.
    Reviews the details of this long friendship - five meetings, the correspondence, and consultations about their writings, which had far-reaching consequences for both men. A chance remark of Southey led Landor to try his hand at Imaginary Conversations - his most successful form. Although Southey appears as a speaker in four Conversations, the voice is that of Landor.

9   STANTON, MICHAEL N. "Southey and the Art of Autobiography." TWC, 5, 113-19.
    Southey's series of autobiographical letters (written between 1820 and 1826) reveal not so much the growth of a mind but rather an attempt to write a minor history of the society which existed in his younger days. His autobiography is not so much a revelation than it is "an exercise in control and selection." The letters are relatively objective, and despite a great deal of information they provide "but little insight into the Southeyan psyche."

10 VOLZ, ROBERT, and JAMES RIEGER. "The Rochester Southey Collection." TWC, 5, 89-91.

1974

>This important collection of Southey manuscripts, begun in 1961, contains over one hundred letters, fourteen poetical manuscripts, and various ephemera.

11 ZALL, P. M. "The Gothic Voice of Father Bear." TWC, 5, 124-28.
>A complete study of "The Story of the Three Bears," a story Southey heard from his Uncle William. A comparison of this tale with contemporary children's literature reveals Southey's artistry as he recreates the improvisational tone of an Uncle William through rhythmical repetition and artful alliteration. Southey did not claim originality: "there is no question that he intended it to celebrate the stories he had heard rather than read in his childhood."

1975 A BOOKS

1 CURRY, KENNETH. Southey. Routledge Author Guide Series. London and Boston: Routledge and Kegan Paul.
>This series, planned for the non-specialist reader, tries to establish "the social and historical context of the writer's life and times, and the cultural and intellectual tradition in which he stands." This study provides an account of Southey's life, his age, and his literary friends, and then discusses his works under the headings of Social and Political Criticism, Biography, Autobiography, Histories, Reviews, Editions, and Translations. The study closes with a discussion of Southey's poetry. The work contains a list of Southey's works and a short bibliography of significant books and articles.

1975 B OTHER WRITINGS

1 CULLER, A. DWIGHT. "Monodrama and the Dramatic Monologue." PMLA, 90, 366-85.
>Places the monodramas of Southey and his contemporaries, William Taylor and Frank Sayers, in the full context of the development of this form.

2 CURRY, KENNETH and ROBERT DEDMON. "Southey's Contributions to the Quarterly Review, TWC, 6, 261-72.
>The first thorough-going attempt to establish an accurate list of Southey's articles for the Quarterly and to discuss those which have been falsely attributed to him. The task of identification has been made difficult by the unreliability - demonstrated in this article - of such presumably reliable sources as the list in Cuthbert Southey's life of

his father and the Contributors' book of the publishing house of Murray.

3   CURRY, KENNETH. "Lamb, Southey, and The Doctor." Charles Lamb Society Bulletin, n.s., no. 10 (April/July), pp. 36-38.
    Brief survey of the Southey-Lamb friendship pointing out the Lamb-like ("Elian") quality of Southey's Doctor, published in the year of Lamb's death (1834) and speculating on how Lamb would have responded to this work.

4   HOFFPAUIR, RICHARD. "The Thematic Structure of Southey's Epic Poetry." TWC, 6, 240-48.
    Southey used themes rather than narrative structure to give unity to his epic narratives: the first, "the necessity for the purgation of evil"; second, "a specifically Romantic and not uncommonly epic hope in a future retreat from heroic and moral duty" in a pastoral setting; and third, "the sanctity of family relations." Although all five of Southey's epics contain these structures, Hoffpauir devotes most of his analysis to Joan of Arc and Thalaba.

5   HORSFALL, NICHOLAS. "Four Unpublished Letters of Robert Southey." N & Q, 220 (September), 399-405.
    Publishes and annotates four letters to Peter Elmsley.

6   MANN, PETER. "Two Unpublished Letters of Robert Southey." N & Q, 22 (September), 397-99.
    Letters to Anna Seward and John Major.

7   RUNYAN, WILLIAM RONALD. "Bob Southey's Diabolical Doggerel: Its Influence on Shelley and Byron." TWC, 6, 249-54.
    Comparative study of Southey's and Coleridge's "The Devil's Thoughts" (1799), Shelley's "The Devil's Walk,"' Byron's "The Devil's Drive," and Southey's expansion of the original stanzas in "The Devil's Walk" (1829). This revision "serves as a grotesque reminder of the reactionary conservatism into which he had settled."

Doctoral Dissertations

1 Bozorth, Richard G. "Robert Southey as a Critic of Poetry." Princeton University, 1951.

2 Comer, David B. "Studies in the Literary Development of Robert Southey." Duke University, 1954.

3 Curry, Kenneth. "The Literary Career of Robert Southey to 1796." Yale University, 1935.

4 Dedmon, Robert A. "The Contributions of Robert Southey to the Quarterly Review, 1809-1839." University of Tennessee, Knoxville, 1975.

5 Early, Benjamin W. "Southey's Joan of Arc: The Unpublished Manuscript, The First Edition, and a Study of the Later Revisions." Duke University, 1951.

6 Geyer, Richard B. "The Literary Reputation of Robert Southey." Northwestern University, 1951.

7 Hager, Philip E. "English Educational Theory and Practice, 1780-1832 As Reflected in the Writings of Wordsworth, Coleridge and Southey." University of Washington, 1951.

8 Haller, William. "The Early Life of Robert Southey, 1774-1803." Columbia University, 1916.

9 Hudson, Charles M., Jr. "The Roderick Legend in English Romantic Literature: Scott, Landor, and Southey." Yale University, 1943.

10 Kaderly, Nathaniel L. "The Later Literary Career of Robert Southey With Particular Reference to His Social Criticism." The Johns Hopkins University, 1952.

11 Kegel, Charles Herbert. "Medieval-Modern Contrasts Used For a Social Purpose in the Work of William Cobbett, Robert Southey, A. Welby Pugin, Thomas Carlyle, John Ruskin, and William Morris." Michigan State University, 1955.

12 Kirkpatrick, Robert Galloway. "The Letters of Robert Southey to Mary Barker From 1800 to 1826." Harvard University, 1967.

13 Kovitz, Miriam G. "The 'Lake Poets': Their Humor." Ohio State University, 1972.

14 Lavelle, John H. "Robert Southey's Thalaba the Destroyer: A New Edition Based Upon the Original Manuscript." New York University, 1973.

15 Longest, Christopher. "Spanish Sources of Southey." University of Chicago, 1915.

16 Manogue, Ralph A. "A Critical Edition of Robert Southey's Wat Tyler." New York University, 1973.

17 McCullough, John W. "Robert Southey's Theories and Concepts of History." University of North Carolina, Chapel Hill, 1951.

18 Marnell, William H. "The Relations of Coleridge and Southey in the Pantisocracy." Harvard University, 1938.

19 Marz, Roy W. "The Poetry and Prose of Robert Southey: A Study in Literary Mediocrity." University of Cincinnati, 1937.

20 Meara, Thomas G. "A Critical Study of the Long Narrative Poems of Robert Southey." Northwestern University, 1956.

21 Ober, Warren Upton. "Lake Poet and Laureate: Southey's Significance to His Own Generation." Indiana University, 1958.

22 Paul-Emile, Barbara Taylor. "Slavery and the English Romantic Poets: Coleridge, Wordsworth and Southey." University of Colorado, 1971.

23 Ramos, Charles. "Letters of Robert Southey to John May 1797-1838." University of Texas at Austin, 1965.

24 Schonert, Vernon Louis. "The Correspondence of Caroline Anne Bowles Southey to Mary Anne Watts Hughes." Harvard University, 1957.

25 Stanton, Michael Neill. "An Edition of the Autobiographical Letters of Robert Southey." University of Rochester, 1972.

26 Thomas, George Stephen. "Wordsworth, Scott, Coleridge, Southey and De Quincey on Catholic Emancipation, 1800-1829: the Conservative Reaction." New York University, 1963.

Doctoral Dissertations

27 Whitney, Daniel R. "The Social and Political Idealism of Robert Southey." Northwestern University, 1950.

28 Whitney, Paul Warren. "Robert Southey's Views on English Literature." University of Pennsylvania, 1960.

29 Wilson, James L. "Folklore in the Long Narrative Poems of Robert Southey." University of North Carolina, Chapel Hill, 1947.

Author/Subject Index

Both authors and subjects are included in this one index. The titles of Southey's individual works and a select group of subject headings pertaining to Southey (such as "bibliography," "biography," and "letters") are listed under Southey's name. Each entry carries a reference to year and entry number. Doctoral dissertations are designated by the letter "D" and will be found in the list of Doctoral Dissertations.

Aikin, John, 1796.B1; 1797.B1
Allchin, A. M., 1958.B1
Anon., 1796.B2; 1797.B2, B3;
    1799.B1; 1801.B1, B2, B3;
    1805.B1, B2; 1807.B1;
    1808.B1; 1809.B1; 1810.B1;
    1811.B1, B2, B3; 1813.B1, B2;
    1814.B1, B2, B3, B5; 1815.B1;
    1817.B1, B2; 1821.B1;
    1822.B1; 1823.B1; 1824.B1,
    B2, B3; 1825.B1, B2; 1829.B1;
    1830.B1; 1844.B1; 1856.B1;
    1864.B1; 1943.B1; 1945.B1
Antippas, Andy P., 1974.B1

Barker, Mary, 1902.B1; 1967D
Barton, Bernard, 1950.B4
Baughman, Roland, 1944.B1
Beaumont, Sir George, 1887.B1
Bedford, Grosvenor Charles,
    1815.B2
Beer, Max, 1919.B1
Bernbaum, Ernest, 1949.B1
Bernhardt-Kabisch, Ernest,
    1974.B2
Betham, Ernest, 1905.B1
Betham, Mary Matilda, 1905.B1
Beyer, W. W., 1963.B1

Blake, William, 1949.B2
Blunt, John James, 1829.B2
Bowles, Caroline. See Caroline
    Bowles Southey
Bowles, William Lisle, 1926.B2;
    1940.B2
Bozorth, Richard G., 1951.D
Braekman, W., 1964.B1
Brightfield, M. F., 1940.B1;
    1944.B2
Brinton, Crane, 1926.B1
Broadus, E. K., 1921.B1
Brooks, Maria Gowen, 1913.A1;
    1926.B3
Brougham, Henry, 1807.B2
Broughton, L. N., 1942.B1
Brown, Simon, 1971.B1
Brown, W. C., 1938.B2
Browne, C. T., 1854.A1
Buceta, Earasmo, 1919.B2; 1922.B1
Butler, H. B., 1911.A1
Byron, George Gordon, Lord,
    1824.B3; 1925.B1; 1932.A1;
    1939.B1; 1953.B2; 1954.B1;
    1960.B2; 1973.B1

Cabral, Adolfo, 1959.A1; 1960.A1
Cahn, Herbert, 1971.A1

Callender, Geoffrey A. R., 1922.A1
Cameron, K. N., 1942.B2
Carlyle, Thomas, 1881.B1; 1905.B3; 1922.B2
Carnall, Geoffrey, 1952.A1; 1955.B1; 1956.B1; 1960.A2; 1964.B2; 1969.B2
Cestre, Charles, 1905.B2
Chambers, R. W., 1925.B1; 1939.B1
Chatterton, Thomas, 1930.B3
Childers, J. S., 1925.A1
Cholmondeley, R. H., 1950.B1
Christie, William D., 1848.B1
Cline, C. L., 1941.B1; 1954.B1
Cobban, Alfred, 1929.A1
Coleridge, E. H., 1889.B1
Coleridge, Hartley, 1829.B3
Coleridge, John Taylor, 1815.B3; 1825.B3
Coleridge, Samuel Taylor, 1817.B3; 1848.B1; 1864.B1; 1895.B1; 1905.B2; 1907.B1; 1917.A1; 1919.B1; 1922.B1; 1925.A2, B1; 1932.B1; 1934.B1; 1939.B2; 1945.B2; 1946.B5; 1949.B4; 1950.B2, B3; 1954.B4; 1959.B2; See also Southey, s. v. pantisocracy
Coleridge, Mrs. Samuel Taylor, 1934.B4
Comer, David B., 1954.D
Conder, Josiah, 1816.B1
Cottle, Joseph, 1847.A1; 1848.B1; 1934.B1; 1970.A1
Croker, John W., 1823.B2; 1940.B1
Culler, A. Dwight, 1975.B1
Curry, Kenneth, 1935.D; 1938.B2; 1939.B2, B3; 1943.B2; 1944.B3; 1948.B1; 1953.B1; 1957.B1; 1961.B1; 1965.A1; 1966.B1; 1967.B1; 1974.B3; 1975.A1, B2, B3

Davis, Bertram R., 1928.B1
Davis, Samuel, 1943.B3
Davy, Humphry, 1858.B1
Davy, John, 1858.B1
Dedmon, Robert, 1975.D; 1975.B2

Dennis, John, 1876.B1; 1887.A1
De Quincey, Thomas, 1839.B1; 1961.A1
Dicey, A. V., 1905.B3
D'Israeli, Isaac, 1941.B1
Dongen, C. Van, 1964.B3
Donne, William B., 1851.B1
Dowden, Edward, 1879.A1; 1881.A1; 1897.B1
Dowden, Wilfred S., 1951.B1
Duppa, Richard, 1938.B2

Early, Benjamin W., 1947.B1; 1951.D
Edmonds, Harry Moreton Southey, 1944.A1
Ehrenpreis, Irvin, 1950.B2
Ehrich, Emil, 1934.A1
Elias, Robert H., 1972.B1
Elliott, Ebenezer, 1939.B4; 1971.B1
Elmsley, Peter, 1975.B5
Elton, Oilver, 1912.B1
Elwin, Malcolm, 1943.B4, B5; 1947.B2
Elwin, Whitwell, 1850.B2; 1956.B2

Fahey, David M., 1966.B2
Fairchild, H. N., 1928.B2; 1931.B1
Feiling, Keith, 1930.B1
Ferriar, John, 1805.B3
Festing, Gabrielle, 1899.B1
FitzGerald, Maurice H., 1909.A1; 1912.A1; 1925.A2; 1930.A1
Fletcher, Ifan Kyrle, 1939.B1
Forster, John, 1869.B1
Foster, John, 1811.B4
Frere, John Hookham, 1899.B1

Gaines, Barry, 1974.B4
George, David, 1971.B2
Geyer, Richard B., 1951.D
Gibbs, W. E., 1934.B1
Gittings, Robert, 1969.A1
Godwin, William, 1905.B2; 1922.B2
Gordan, J. D., 1963.B2
Graham, Walter, 1923.B1

Author/Subject Index

Grannis, Ruth S., 1913.A1
Greever, Garland, 1926.B2
Griggs, Earl L., 1932.B1; 1945.B2
Griggs, Irwin, 1945.B4
Grigson, Geoffrey, 1970.A2

Hager, Philip E., 1951.D
Haller, William, 1916.D; 1917.A1; 1922.B2
Hannay, David, 1895.B1
Harvey, E. R. H., 1953.A1
Havens, Raymond D., 1929.B2; 1932.B2; 1945.B3; 1946.B1
Hayden, John O., 1969.B3
Hazlitt, William, 1816.B2; 1817.B4; 1825.B4; 1930.B2
Heber, Reginald, 1810.B2; 1817.B5; 1820.B1
Heber, Richard (and Heber Family) 1950.B1
Heraud, Edith, 1898.B1
Heraud, John, 1898.B1
Herford, C. H., 1929.A1
Hoadley, Frank T., 1941.B2
Hoffpauir, Richard, 1975.B4
Hopkins, Kenneth, 1954.B2
Horsfall, Nicholas, 1975.B5
Howe, H. W., 1943.B6
Hudson, Charles M., Jr., 1943.D

Irving, Washington, 1946.B6

Jacobus, Mary, 1971.B3
Jarrett-Kerr, Martin, 1942.B3
Jeffery, Sidney, 1943.B7
Jeffrey, Francis, 1802.B1; 1805.B4; 1808.B3; 1811.B5; 1814.B4; 1815.B4; 1816.B3; 1817.B6; 1821.B2
Jerdan, William, 1866.B1

Kaderly, N. L., 1952.D; 1954.B3; 1955.B2
Kaufman, P., 1924.B1
Keats, John, 1898.B1; 1961.B2
Kegel, Charles Herbert, 1955.D
Kern, J. D., 1945.B4

Keynes, Geoffrey, 1949.B2
King, R. W., 1956.B2
Kirkpatrick, Robert G., 1967.D
Knight, William, 1887.B1
Knowlton, E. C., 1928.B3; 1929.B3
Kovitz, Miriam G., 1972.D
Kroeber, Karl, 1966.B3

Lachmann, V. R., 1946.B4
Lamb, Charles, 1917.A1; 1965.B1; 1975.B3
Landor, Walter Savage, 1850.B1; 1869.B1; 1927.B1; 1934.A1; 1954.B5; 1974.B7
Lavelle, John H., 1973.D
Lewis, N. B., 1934.B2
Lister, Thomas H., 1831.B1
Llorens, Vicente, 1972.B2
Lockhart, John G., 1824.B4; 1831.B2; 1834.B1, B2; 1843.B1; 1850.B2
Logan, Sister Eugenia, 1930.B3
Longest, Christopher, 1915.D
Lope de Vega, 1922.B1
Lounsbury, T. R., 1915.B1

Mabbott, T. O., 1926.B3
Macaulay, Rose, 1946.B2
Macaulay, Thomas B., 1830.B1; 1831.B3; 1902.B2; 1922.B2
McCullough, John W., 1951.D
McElderry, B. R., Jr., 1955.B3
MacGillivray, J. B., 1931.B2
Madden, Lionel, 1972.A1
Major, John, 1975.B6
Mann, Peter, 1975.B6
Manogue, Ralph A., 1973.D
Marcus, H., 1932.B3
Marnell, William H., 1938.D
Marples, Morris, 1967.B2
Martin, C. G., 1967.B3; 1970.B1
Martin, Richard T., 1966.B4
May, John, 1965.D
Meara, Thomas G., 1956.D
Merchant, Paul, 1969.B4
Merivale, Herman, 1836.B1; 1839.B2
Merivale, John Herman, 1815.B5
Metzdorf, R. F., 1956.B3; 1959.B1

Meyerstein, E. H. W., 1930.B4
Mill, James, 1825.B5
Montgomery, James, 1815.B6
Montluzin, Emily Lorraine De, 1973.B1
Moody, Christopher L., 1808.B4
Moore, Thomas, 1969.B2; 1973.B1
Morgan, Peter F., 1971.B4; 1974.B5
Morley, Edith J., 1927.B2; 1938.B3
Murray, John, 1891.B1

Nicoll, W. R., 1902.A1
Nowell-Smith, Simon, 1965.B1

Ober, Kenneth H., 1965.B2; 1974.B7
Ober, Warren U., 1958.D; 1958.B2; 1959.B2; 1965.B2; 1968.B1; 1974.B7
"Olybrius," 1934.B3
Oman, Carola, 1962.A1

Park, Roy, 1974.B7
Parker, W. M., 1960.B1
Partington, Wilfred, 1930.B5
Patterson, C. I., 1961.B2
Paul-Emile, Barbara Taylor, 1971.D
Peardon, T. P., 1933.B1
Peck, Walter E., 1927.B3
Pfandl, Ludwig, 1913.B1
Pollin, B. R., 1968.B2; 1969.B5
Potter, Stephen, 1934.B4
Pritchett, V. S., 1958.A1
Procter, George, 1823.B2
Proudfit, Charles L., 1974.B8

Raimond, Jean, 1968.A1
Ramamurty, K., 1969.B6
Ramos, Charles, 1965.D
Reed, Joseph W., Jr., 1966.B5
Renwick, W. L., 1940.B2
Richter, Helene, 1929.B4
Rickman, John, 1911.B1; 1929.A1; 1955.B2

Rieger, James, 1974.B10
Robberds, J. W., 1843.B1
Roberts, R. Ellis, 1932.A1
Robinson, Henry Crabb, 1869.B2; 1927.B2; 1938.B3
Rogers, Fred, 1973.B2
Runyan, William R., 1975.B7

Sadler, Thomas, 1869.B2
St. Barbe, Roger F., 1830.B3
Saintsbury, George, 1895.B1; 1914.B1; 1923.B2
Sanderson, David R., 1971.B5
Schilling, B. N., 1946.B3
Schneider, Elisabeth, 1945.B4
Schonert, Vernon Louis, 1957.D
Schrickx, W., 1956.B5
Scott, Harold Spencer, 1902.B1
Scott, Sir Walter, 1803.B2; 1804.B1; 1809.B2; 1811.B6; 1830.B4; 1834.B2; 1930.B5
Seary, E. R., 1939.B4
Selig, K. L., 1956.B4
Seronsy, C. C., 1954.B4
Seton, Barbara, 1937.B1
Seward, Anna, 1975.B6
Shamburger, M. I., 1946.B4
Shand, John, 1943.B8
Shaver, Chester L., 1960.B2
Shelley, Percy Bysshe, 1881.A1; 1925.B1; 1927.B3; 1942.B2; 1943.B4; 1953.B2; 1956.B2
Shine, Hill and Helen, 1949.B3
Shuman, R. Baird, 1961.B3
Simmons, Jack, 1945.A1; 1951.A1
Smiles, Samuel, 1891.B1
Sousa-Leao, J. de, 1943.B9, B10
Southey, Caroline Bowles, 1866.B1; 1881.A1; 1926.B2; 1957.D
Southey, Charles Cuthbert, 1849.B1; 1850.B1; 1851.B1
Southey, Robert (Titles of individual works and selected general topics)
All for Love, 1829.B3
Amadis of Gaul, 1803.B1, B2; 1913.B1
Annual Anthology, 1799.B1; 1800.B1; 1858.B1; 1948.B1
Annual Review, 1939.B3; 1960.A2; 1973.B1

Author/Subject Index

Ballads, 1909.B1; 1913.B1; 1919.B2; 1965.B2; 1968.B2; 1969.B2, B4, B5; 1974.B6
Bibliography (including additions to the Southey canon), 1918.B1; 1926.B3; 1932.B2, B3; 1934.B3; 1938.B2; 1939.B3; 1948.B1; 1949.B1; 1953.B1; 1955.B3; 1956.B3; 1957.B1; 1959.B1; 1963.B2; 1966.B1; 1967.B1; 1969.B1; 1971.B2; 1972.A1; 1974.B9; 1975.B2
Biography, 1850.B2; 1854.A1; 1857.B1; 1866.B1; 1879.A1; 1911.B1; 1914.B1; 1917.A1; 1926.B2; 1929.B4; 1934.B4; 1938.B3; 1943.B1, B5, B6; 1945.A1, B1; 1947.B2; 1954.B5; 1964.B2; 1968.A1; 1975.A1
Book of the Church, 1824.B1, B2; 1825.B5
Books and Book Collecting (Southey's Library), 1839.B1; 1844.B1; 1864.B1; 1924.B1; 1943.B9; 1949.B4; 1950.B1; 1956.B4; 1961.B1; 1966.B4; 1974.B7
Bunyan (Southey's edition of and life of), 1830.B4; 1831.B3
Carmen Nuptiale, 1816.B2, B3
Carmen Triumphale, 1814.B1, B2, B3, B4
Chatterton's Works (edited with Joseph Cottle), 1804.B1; 1930.B4
Chronicle of the Cid, 1808.B1; 1809.B1, B2; 1825.B1; 1913.B1; 1958.A1
Colloquies, see Sir Thomas More
Cowper (Southey's edition of and life of), 1836.B1
Critical Review, 1918.B1
The Curse of Kehama, 1811.B1, B3, B4, B5, B6; 1895.B1
"The Devil's Walk," 1975.B5
The Doctor, 1834.B1; 1835.B1; 1914.B1; 1930.A1; 1956.B4; 1975.B3

Eclogues, 1928.B2, B3; 1975.B1
Edinburgh Annual Register, 1960.A2
Edinburgh Review, 1802.B1; 1830.B1; 1932.B1; 1960.B2; 1969.B3
Essays (1832), 1922.B2
"The Exiled Patriots," 1932.B3; 1954.B4
An Exposure of the Misrepresentations and Calumnies in Mr. Marsh's Review of Sir George Barlow's Administration at Madras, 1953.B1
Foreign Quarterly Review, 1932.B2
Foreign Review, 1932.B2
Histories, 1876.B1; 1915.B1; 1933.B1; 1951.D
The History of Brazil, 1810.B1; 1811.B2; 1817.B1, B5; 1876.B1; 1916.A1; 1933.B1; 1943.B10; 1971.A1
The History of the Peninsular War, 1822.B1; 1823.B1, B2
Joan of Arc, 1796.B1, B2; 1825.B1; 1864.B1; 1905.B2; 1917.A1; 1947.B1; 1951.D; 1965.B1; 1975.B4
Journal of a Tour in Scotland, 1929.A1
Journal of a Tour in the Netherlands in the Autumn of 1815, 1902.A1
Laureateship, 1921.B1; 1954.B2
Lay of the Laureate, 1816.B2, B3
A Letter to William Smith, 1817.B6
Letters, 1847.A1; 1849.A1; 1850.B2; 1856.A1, B2; 1858.B1; 1860.B1; 1869.B1, B2; 1876.B1; 1881.A1; 1887.A1, B1; 1889.B1; 1891.B1; 1898.B1; 1899.B1; 1902.B1, B2; 1905.B1; 1911.B1; 1912.A1; 1927.B1;

1930.B4; 1932.B1; 1934.B2;
1937.B1; 1939.B3; 1940.B1,
B2; 1941.B1; 1942.B1;
1943.B7, B9; 1944.B4;
1945.B2; 1950.B1, B2, B4;
1954.B1; 1956.B5; 1960.B2;
1961.B3; 1964.B1; 1965.A1;
1967.B1, B3; 1970.B1;
1972.B2; 1974.B1, B8;
1975.B5, B6
Letters from England by Don
  Manuel Espriella, 1807.B3;
  1808.B3, B4; 1916.A1;
  1951.A1; 1954.B3
Letters Written During a
  Short Residence in Spain
  and Portugal, 1797.B3;
  1959.A1; 1960.A1
The Life of Nelson, 1813.B1,
  B2; 1911.A1; 1922.A1;
  1953.A1; 1962.A1; 1966.B5
The Life of Wesley, 1820.A1,
  B1; 1824.B4; 1925.A2;
  1933.B1; 1943.B3; 1946.B1
Literary Criticism, 1971.B4;
  1974.B5
The Lives and Works of the
Uneducated Poets, 1831.B1,
  B2; 1925.A1
The Lives of the British Admirals, 1895.A1
Madoc, 1805.B1, B2, B3, B4,
  B5, B6; 1817.B1; 1895.B1;
  1909.B1; 1913.B1; 1934.A1;
  1943.D
Metrical Tales, 1805.B7
Malory's Morte D'Arthur
  (Southey's edition),
  1974.B4
"Mohammed," 1958.B2
Molina's Geographical, Natural, and Civil History of
  Chili, 1953.B1
Monodramas, 1929.B3; 1975.B1
Morning Post, 1889.B1;
  1955.B3; 1956.B1; 1971.B3
Observer, 1928.B1
Odes to his Royal Highness
  the Prince Regent....,
  1814.B5
Omniana, 1954.B3; 1969.A1

The Origin, Nature and Object
  of the New System of Education, 1972.A2
Palmerin of England, 1808.B2;
  1814.B5; 1913.B1; 1961.B2
Pantisocracy, 1905.B2;
  1917.A1; 1930.B3; 1931.B1,
  B2; 1933.B2; 1938.D
The Pilgrim of Compostella,
  1829.B3
Poems (1797), 1797.B1, B2
Poetical Works (1837-38),
  1839.B2
A Poet's Pilgrimage, 1816.B1
Portraits (of Southey),
  1974.B3
Portugal and Portuguese
  Studies, 1899.B1; 1913.B1;
  1927.B4; 1943.B10; 1946.B2;
  1959.A1; 1960.A1
Quarterly Review, 1825.B1;
  1881.B1; 1891.B1; 1916.A1;
  1922.B2; 1923.B1; 1943.B5;
  1944.B2; 1945.B4; 1949.B3;
  1955.B2; 1960.B2, B1;
  1966.B2; 1971.B1; 1975.D;
  1975.B2
Religious Opinions, 1952.B1;
  1955.B1; 1958.B1; 1960.A2
Roderick, 1815.B1, B2, B3, B4,
  B5, B6; 1817.B1; 1895.B1;
  1909.B1; 1913.B1; 1934.A1;
  1943.D
Scandinavia, 1932.B4
Sir Thomas More; or Colloquies on the Progress and
  Prospects of Society,
  1829.B1, B2; 1830.B1, B2;
  1897.B1; 1911.B1; 1916.A1;
  1922.B2; 1942.B3; 1958.B1,
  B3
Spanish Literature, 1913.B1;
  1915.D; 1919.B2; 1922.B1
Specimens of the Later English Poets, 1807.B1, B2;
  1945.B3
"The Story of the Three
  Bears," 1902.B2; 1946.B4;
  1951.B2; 1968.B1; 1973.B2;
  1974.B11
A Tale of Paraguay, 1825.B1,
  B2, B3; 1974.B2

Author/Subject Index

Thalaba, 1801.B2, B3; 1802.B1; 1803.B3; 1850.B2; 1917.A1; 1938.B1; 1951.B1; 1963.B1; 1973.D; 1975.B4
Vindiciae Ecclesiae Anglicanae, 1830.B3
A Vision of Judgment, 1821.B1, B2; 1932.A1
Wat Tyler, 1817.B2, B3, B6; 1905.B2; 1941.B2; 1953.B2; 1973.D
Westminster School, 1944.B1; 1967.B2
Stanton, Michael N., 1972.D, B1; 1974.B9
Starr, N. C., 1946.B5
Stephen, Leslie, 1902.B2
Stuart, Daniel, 1889.B1
Super, R. H., 1954.B5
Symons, Arthur, 1909.B1

Taylor, William, 1803.B3; 1805.B5, B6, B7; 1807.B3; 1843.B1, B2; 1848.B1
Telford, Thomas, 1929.A1
Thackeray, W. M., 1860.B1
Thom, J. H., 1845.B1
Thomas, George Stephen, 1963.D
Tilney, Chrystal, 1968.B3
Tolstoy, Leo, 1968.B1
Tuckerman, Henry T., 1857.B1; 1860.A1

Volz, 1974.B10

Walter, Félix, 1927.B4
Ward, William S., 1972.B3
Warter, John W., 1856.A1
Watson, Richard, 1820.A1
Weber, C. A., 1935.B1
Whalley, George, 1949.B4; 1950.B3
White, Joseph Blanco, 1845.B1; 1972.B2
Whitney, Daniel R., 1950.D
Whitney, Paul Warren, 1960.D
Williams, Orlo, 1911.B2
Williams, Raymond, 1958.B3
Wilson, J. L., 1946.B6; 1947.D
Wilson, John, 1835.B1
Woodring, Carl R., 1950.B4
Wordsworth, William, 1802.B1; 1839.B1; 1905.B2; 1917.B1; 1919.B1; 1929.B2; 1938.B2; 1942.B1; 1944.B3; 1955.B3; 1956.B1; 1960.B2; 1970.B3
Wright, H. G., 1932.B4; 1933.B2

Zall, P. M., 1953.B2; 1974.B11
Zandvoort, R. W., 1944.B4
Zeitlin, Jacob, 1916.A1; 1918.B1
Žukovskij, 1965.B2; 1974.B6